A Student Handbook for
Writing in Biology
Stony Brook University Edition

A Student Handbook for Writing in Biology

Writing in Biology

STONY BROOK UNIVERSITY EDITION

Karin Knisely

Bucknell University

Marvin H. O'Neal III, Ph.D.

Stony Brook University

SINAUER ASSOCIATES, INC.

W. H. FREEMAN AND COMPANY

Cover photos:
Flower: *Semi-cactus Dahlia*; photo by Andrew Sinauer.
Frog: *orange-eyed tree frog*, Litoria sp.; Parrot: *scarlet macaw,* Ara macao; Tortoise: *Aldabra Island giant tortoise*, Geocholone Gigantea; photos by Gerry Ellis/Digital Vision.

Address editorial correspondence to:
Sinauer Associates, Inc., 23 Plumtree Road, Sunderland, Massachusetts 01375 U.S.A.
www.sinauer.com

ISBN-13: 978-1-4292-2941-8

Printed in Canada

To those who go the extra mile in pursuit of excellence

Contents

CHAPTER 5 *Revision 63*

CHAPTER 6 *A "Good" Sample Student Laboratory Report 95*

CHAPTER 7 *Poster Presentations 109*

PREFACE

The goal of this handbook is to provide students with a practical, readable resource for communicating their scientific knowledge according to the conventions in biology. However, these are just guidelines. You will most likely encounter many different types of guidelines in your other courses. When you begin submitting your own work for publication in scientific journals, you will see that each journal has its own set of rules. For example, the journal *Science* places methods in the reference section. But whether you are writing for Science or preparing a Stony Brook lab report, writing in biology requires a variety of skills which include

- Understanding the scientific method (Chapter 1)
- Locating pertinent sources efficiently (Chapter 2)
- Learning to read scientific journal articles and paraphrasing the main ideas, not only to avoid plagiarism, but also to improve comprehension (Chapter 3)
- Describing scientific work in the appropriate format, tone, and style (Chapter 4)
- Writing multiple drafts of papers and revising for clarity and conciseness (Chapter 5)
- Getting feedback from peer reviewers and instructors in a timely fashion and paying attention to mistakes to avoid repeating them in subsequent papers (Chapter 6)
- Becoming proficient at using word processing, computer-graphing, and presentation graphics programs (Appendices 1, 2, and 3).

Besides writing about it, we communicate scientific knowledge through posters and oral presentations. In these forms of communication, however, visuals and the speaker's delivery play a greater role than the written material in conveying the message. Tips on preparing good posters are given in Chapter 7. Guidelines for effective oral presentations (Chapter 8) and step-by-step instructions for preparing oral presentations in MS PowerPoint (Appendix 3) are new to the Second Edition.

Furthermore, the Second Edition has been revised and reorganized to increase user-friendliness. The technology sections (Chapter 2 on biology databases, Appendices 1 and 2 on Microsoft Word and Excel) have been updated. To illustrate basic principles for formatting graphs and tables, visuals have been added to complement the textual description. To help students decide on what kind of visual (graph or table) best summarizes their results, data from actual lab exercises are presented with explanations for possible ways to organize the data. Finally, the First Edition's Appendix 4 on faulty writing has been streamlined and incorporated into Chapters 4 and 5. Examples (along with revisions) illustrate typical kinds of mistakes found in different sections of a laboratory report.

Two checklists, **Biology Laboratory Report Checklist** and **Laboratory Report Mistakes**, are included in this text for use in both the revision and feedback stages. Students and peer reviewers can focus on specific points in order to evaluate lab report drafts critically. Instructors may save time providing feedback by using the Checklist for general content and style considerations and the Mistakes key for more specific feedback. Instead of writing a detailed explanation of an error, the instructor may simply write a number corresponding to an entry in the key; it is then the student's responsibility to consult the key for the number's meaning.

Acknowledgments

Feedback from users of the First Edition guided changes made in the Second Edition. In particular, I would like to thank my students in Introduction to Molecules and Cells and Organismal Biology laboratories for giving me suggestions on how to improve this book. The following comment exemplifies the attitude of many first and second-year biology students toward writing, and makes me smile: "I don't enjoy writing lab reports, but your book was extremely helpful in doing so." My colleagues in the Biology Department at Bucknell continue to contribute both a pleasant work environment and valuable feedback on content and readability. I also appreciate the help of Bucknell's Information Services & Resources staff in answering my research and computer-related questions. Special thanks go to Walter H. Piper (Chapman University) for his thoughtful comments on the use of passive and active voice, Warren Abrahamson (Bucknell University) for helping me clarify the use of trendlines, and Karen Patrias (National Library of Medicine) for her insight on citation and reference styles.

I am grateful to all the professionals at Sinauer Associates and W.H. Freeman who helped with the production of this book, especially Andy

Sinauer and Sara Tenney, who provided encouragement, feedback, and organizational input on both the First and Second Editions. Carol Wigg and Chelsea Holabird meticulously guided the book through the editorial and production processes and Joanne Delphia incorporated the visuals in an attractive layout. Jefferson Johnson deserves the credit for the cool cover and Jason Dirks and Parker Morse set up the website for the ancillary materials.

I also express my sincere appreciation to those who contributed to the First Edition: John Woolsey (poster presentations), Lynne Waldman (good student lab report), Joe Parsons (University of Victoria), Randy Wayne (Cornell University), John Byram (W.W. Norton & Co.), Kristy Sprott (The Format Group LLC), Wendy Sera (Baylor University), Elizabeth Bowdan (University of Massachusetts at Amherst), Mary Been (Clovis Community College), and the staff of the Bucknell Writing Center.

My passions outside of teaching biology helped shape the style and content of this book. I have always loved sports and, for the past three years, have helped coach the Central Susquehanna girls' lacrosse team. Just as coaching and teaching go hand in hand, excelling on the playing field and in the classroom both require preparation, discipline, teamwork, and a willingness to do one's best. Through lacrosse, I have had the privilege of meeting players, parents, coaches, and umpires who have helped me become a better teacher and coach.

As a freelance German to English technical translator, I appreciate the challenge of choosing just the right words to communicate information faithfully, in a clear and concise manner, and according to conventions familiar to the reader. I am indebted to the translation profession for setting high standards of quality. While the process of writing in a particular genre is challenging, it is also immensely satisfying: We experience the joy of learning, the pleasure of sharing our knowledge with others, and the creativity involved in putting thoughts into words. Especially rewarding is the enthusiasm we generate when we communicate our knowledge well.

Lastly, I would like to thank my family and friends for their unwavering encouragement and love. I am especially grateful to my parents, Elfriede and Adolph Wegener, who have been excellent role models, and who have instilled in me a love of languages and given me a positive outlook on life. My children, Katrina, Carleton, and Brian, continue to be my pride and joy. I would not be able to pursue all of my passions without the support of my husband, Chuck, whose love and sense of humor sustain me.

KARIN KNISELY
LEWISBURG, PA
OCTOBER 2004

The Second Edition of A Student Handbook for Writing in Biology was well organized, concise, and contained the vast majority of the content presented in this edition. The principal modifications contributed to this outstanding and highly useful text were topics important for our students here at Stony Brook University and include an update of instructions for the use of Microsoft Office. Our campus recently switched to Office 2007 and at least for us, this new software was not intuitively obvious. Someone had to learn the intricacies of this important software and explain it to the rest of us. That "someone" became two, Kelly L. O'Donnell and Rocio S. Ng who took on this arduous task, and we have greatly benefited from their extraordinary efforts. The topical additions for Stony Brook students are the result of the insight and expertise of Joan M. Miyazaki and Deborah Spikes, who have made yet another project enjoyable and successful.

I echo Karin Knisely's appreciation and thanks for the hard work of the professionals at Sinauer Associates and W.H. Freeman in the preparation of this text, especially Kathaleen Emerson, who edited this edition, Joan Gemme, who paged the book and was ably assisted by Joanne Delphia, Janice Holabird, and Jefferson Johnson. A special thanks to Christopher Small, who kept us focused and on track.

This SBU edition is the result of many dedicated and talented individuals; it has been a pleasure working with all of you.

MARVIN H. O'NEAL III
STONY BROOK, NY
JUNE 2008

Chapter 1

THE SCIENTIFIC METHOD

Trying to understand natural phenomena is human nature. We are curious about why things happen the way they do, and we expect to be able to understand these events through careful observation and measurement. This is known as the **scientific method**, and it is the foundation of all knowledge in the biological sciences.

An Introduction to the Scientific Method

The scientific method involves a number of steps:

1. Ask a question
2. Look for sources that might help answer the question
3. Develop a possible explanation (hypothesis)
4. Design an experiment to test the hypothesis
5. Predict what the outcome of an experiment will be based on the hypothesis
6. Collect data
7. Organize data to better interpret the results
8. Develop possible explanations for the experimental results
9. Revise the original hypothesis taking into account new findings and design new experiments to test new hypotheses
10. Share findings with other scientists

Most scientists do not rigidly adhere to this sequence of steps, but it provides a useful starting point for how to conduct a scientific investigation.

1. Ask a Question

As a biology student, you are probably naturally curious about your environment. You wonder about the hows and whys of things you observe. To apply the scientific method to your questions, however, the phenomena of interest must be sufficiently well defined. The parameters that describe the phenomena must be measurable and controllable. For example, let's say that you made the following observation:

> Dwarf pea plants contain a lower concentration of the hormone gibberellic acid than wild-type pea plants of normal height.

To change this observation into a quiestion you might ask:

> Does gibberellic acid regulate plant height?

This question can be answered using the scientific method, because the parameters can be controlled and measured. On the other hand, the following question could not be answered easily with the scientific method:

> Will the addition of gibberellic acid make a plant happy?

In this example, "plant happiness" is not something that can be measured or controlled.

2. Look for Answers to Your Question

There is a good chance that other people have already asked and tried to answer the same question you have asked. So you may be able to find an answer to your question, if you know where to look. Textbooks, journal articles, and the Internet (see Harnack and Kleppinger, 2001 for ways to determine a website's reliability) are good places to begin finding answers. Attempts to answer the original question often result in new questions and unexpected findings lead to new directions in research. Other people's ideas may lead you to think of a more interesting question, define your question more clearly, or modify your question in some other way.

3. Turn Your Question into a Hypothesis

As a result of your literature search or conversations with experts, you may develop a tentative answer to your original (or modified) question. Now it is time to develop a hypothesis. A **hypothesis** is a possible explanation for something you have observed. **You must have infor-**

mation before you can propose a hypothesis! Without information, your hypothesis is nothing more than an uneducated guess. This is why you must look for possible answers before you can turn your question into a hypothesis.

A useful hypothesis can be tested and either supported or negated. A hypothesis is never "proven" right, but the evidence gained from your observations and/or measurements can provide support for the hypothesis. Thus, when biologists write papers, they never say, "The results prove that… ." Instead, they write, "The results suggest that…" or "The results provide support for… ."

You might transform your question "Does gibberellic acid regulate plant height?" into the following hypothesis:

> The addition of gibberellic acid to dwarf plants will allow them to grow to the height of normal, wild-type plants.

4. Design an Experiment to Test Your Hypothesis

It doesn't matter whether your hypothesis ultimately is wrong or unsupported. A hypothesis is simply a starting point for designing an experiment to test your explanation. Designing experiments requires experience, creativity, and a sense for what is practical. Experience may be gained from reading methods published by others and modifying them to suit your purpose. Creativity involves brainstorming to view the subject from many different perspectives. A sense for what is practical is required, because your experimental design will be limited by considerations such as availability of equipment and supplies, cost, time, and so on.

When you design an experiment, pay attention to the following points.

Define the variables. There are three general kinds of variables: dependent variables, the independent variable, and controlled variables. **Dependent variables** are variables such as growth, number of seeds, number of body segments, number of offspring, and so on that you can measure or observe. These variables may be altered by the experimental conditions.

The *one* variable that a scientist manipulates in a given experiment is called the **independent variable**. In a different experiment, a different independent variable can be manipulated. It is important to have *only one* independent variable in a given experiment, because otherwise you don't know which factor is affecting the dependent variable(s).

There are many variables that could possibly affect the outcome of an experiment. Thus, it is important to vary only one (the independent variable) and to keep all others constant. The ones that remain constant are called the **controlled variables**. If, for example, you decide to investigate the effect of gibberellic acid on plant growth, variables such as temperature, humidity, age of the plants, day length, amount of fertilizer, watering regime, and so on would all have to be kept constant. These are the controlled variables.

Design the procedure. Determine how you will carry out your experiment. You might base your procedure on articles from scientific journals, suggestions from colleagues, intuition or experience, or simply the desire to try out a new idea. The procedure typically includes the following components.

- **Control treatment.** This is the condition that serves as a reference for the test treatments. Controls are important because they help to demonstrate whether or not your treatment variables are responsible for your experimental outcomes. Experiments may have both positive and negative control treatments, as illustrated by the following example:

  Hypothesis: The addition of gibberellic acid to dwarf plants will allow them to grow to the height of normal, wild-type plants.

  Negative control: Dwarf plants not given gibberellic acid.

  Positive control: Normal plants not given gibberellic acid.

- **Level of treatment for independent variable.** What concentration of gibberellic acid should be tested? We don't want to choose a concentration that is too low, otherwise we might not see any effect. On the other hand, the concentration should not be so high that it is toxic to the plant. The level of treatment is usually based on previous research (journal articles) or preliminary experiments. The level can even be a range that is appropriate for the biological system or organism to be tested.

- **Replication.** A single result is not statistically valid. The experiment must be repeated several times to see whether similar results are found. The results from several trials may be averaged and analyzed using statistical tests.

5. Make Predictions about the Outcome of Your Experiment

Before you carry out your experiment, you should have some idea of what results to expect if your hypothesis is correct. Making predictions involves **inductive reasoning**, whereby you use general knowledge or experience to predict the outcome of a specific experiment. For the previous example, you might predict the following results:

- **Test treatment:** Dwarf plants should grow taller when they are treated with water containing gibberellic acid.

- **Negative control:** Dwarf plants treated with plain water should remain short (i.e., the solvent for gibberellic acid is water).

- **Postive control:** Wild-type (normal plants) treated with plain water should reach their normal, tall height.

If the outcome of the experiments matches your predictions, then your hypothesis is supported. If not, then your hypothesis is refuted, and you may wish to repeat the experiment, double-check your experimental set-up, and/or come up with a different hypothesis.

Predictions are an important tool, because they give you a sense of direction. But there is a danger here, too: Never let your predictions affect your objectivity. **Do not make your results fit your predictions—** instead, modify your hypothesis and experiment again.

What is learned from a **negated** hypothesis can be just as valuable as what is learned from a "successful" experiment. The subsequent modifications of the hypothesis and the associated experiments help researchers gain assurance that their explanation of a particular phenomenon is reasonable and valid.

6. Collect Data

Once you have planned and set up your experiment, you are ready to make observations or measurements about your test subject. Consistency is very important in this regard. If, for example, you are measuring plant height, you must always measure according to the same criteria. If you measure from the rim of the pot to the shoot tip the first time, you can't measure from the soil to the shoot tip the next time without introducing error into the results. Sometimes it is necessary to modify during the course of your experiment *how* you collect data and *what kinds of data* are important. These modifications may also be included when you design your next experiment.

You should realize that even some of the most elementary questions in biology have taken hundreds of scientists many years to answer. One approach to the problem may seem promising at first, but as data are collected, problems with the method or other complications may become apparent. Although the scientific method is indeed methodical, it also requires imagination and creativity. Successful scientists are not discouraged when their initial hypotheses are discredited. Instead, they are already revising their hypotheses in light of recent discoveries and planning their next experiment. You usually will not get instant gratification from applying the scientific method to a question, but your patience is more likely to be rewarded with unexpected findings, and a greater appreciation for the complexity of biological phenomena.

How to handle variability and unexpected results. Variability is a fact of life. If you toss a coin 10 times, you may get 5 heads and 5 tails the first time, 4 heads and 6 tails the second time, and 8 heads and 2 tails the third time. Even though you used the same coin and tossed it the same way, you got different results in different trials.

This same kind of variability is likely to be present in experimental data. Even when you apply the same treatment to different plants of the same species, the individual plants may respond differently, and even the same individual may not respond the same way to the same treatment twice. How do you know if the different results are due to variability among individuals, the imprecision in making measurements, or some other factor?

This is where statistical analysis comes in. Statistics can help you determine how far you can trust the results when you are sampling a subset of a population in which individuals differ. Statistics can help you decide if the different measurements you obtained for replicates are significant or not.

Some common statistical tests and their uses are given in Table 1.1. Consult a good statistics text (see the Bibliography: Samuels and Witner, 1999; Moore, 2000; Utts and Heckard, 2002) for details on the different tests.

TABLE 1.1 Common statistical tests and their uses

TEST	APPLICATION
Chi square	To compare how closely the observed or measured data compare to the expected results (e.g., for crosses in genetics)
t-test	To compare the means of two groups
ANOVA	To compare the means of three or more groups

What if your results cannot be explained by variability? Although you would like to give yourself the benefit of the doubt, human error is a possibility, especially in introductory biology laboratory exercises. Human error includes failure to follow the procedure, failure to use the equipment properly, failure to prepare solutions correctly, variability when multiple lab partners measure the same thing, and simple arithmetic errors. If you suspect that human error may have influenced your results, it is important to acknowledge its contribution, but only if you are able to explain why. If you had time to repeat the experiment, you would first try to eliminate sources of human error rather than revise your original hypothesis.

7. Organize the Data

Raw data must be summarized and organized before you can begin any interpretation. Data is commonly organized into tables, graphs, and figures because they help make data easier to interpret. Tables have rows and columns and are useful for displaying several dependent variables at the same time or when you want to emphasize the numbers themselves rather than the trend shown by the numbers. Figures are graphs, pictures, diagrams, gel photos, X-ray images, and microscope images—any visual that is not a table.

Line graphs and bar graphs are commonly used in data analysis. **Line graphs** show the effect of the independent variable (the one the scientist manipulates) on a selected dependent variable (the one that changes in response to the independent variable). By convention, the independent variable is plotted on the x-axis, and the dependent variable is plotted on the y-axis. Let's say that for 3 weeks, you treated dwarf and normal plant groups as described under "Predictions" (page 5). If you choose to summarize your results in a line graph, plot time on the x-axis, because time is the variable you controlled. Plot height on the y-axis, because this is the variable you expect to change over time, depending on the treatment.

Bar graphs allow you to compare individual sets of data when the data are *discontinuous* (e.g., male versus female or high versus low nutrients). In the previous example, if you wanted to compare the final heights of the plants in the different treatment groups, each bar would represent the height of one group of plants at the end of the 3-week period. The data are discontinuous because different treatment groups are being compared.

The best way to display the data depends on the point you are trying to make. For example, if you want to show that the rate of growth is faster in plants treated with gibberellic acid than that in untreated plants, then a line graph would work well. If you want to emphasize that the end effect of treating plants with gibberellic acid is a taller plant, then a bar graph would be suitable. If you want to compare the actual heights of your plants with those in the literature, then a table would be useful. Also keep in mind that a "picture is worth a thousand words," especially when you are comparing physical differences like height, color, and overall appearance of the organisms. Photographs may call your attention to variables that you didn't measure, but that you might want to consider in future experiments. Photographs are also very effective in poster presentations.

The process of summarizing and organizing data initially involves trial and error, especially when you have a lot of data, the results are variable or unexpected, or you do not have a clear understanding of the purpose of the experiment. These difficulties are a normal part of the learning curve; your organizational ability will improve with practice and experience. See the section on "Organizing Your Data" in Chapter 4 as a starting point.

Regardless of how you choose to display the data, you must be honest. Do not exaggerate axes or trends to support your hypothesis when, in truth, the data do not support it. Show variability when necessary. Use statistical methods to reduce huge amounts of data, and be prepared to explain your reasoning.

Keep in mind that there may be *no difference* between the control and the experimental treatments. If there was no difference, say so, and then try to develop possible explanations for these results.

8. Try to Explain the Results

Once you have organized the data, you are ready to develop possible explanations for the results. You already found sources on the topic when you developed your hypothesis. Return to this material to try to explain your results. Do your results agree with the findings of other researchers? Do you agree with their explanations? If your results do not agree, try to determine why not. Were different methods, organisms, or conditions employed? What were some possible sources of error?

9. Revise Original Hypothesis and Design New Experiments

If the data support the hypothesis, then you should suggest additional experiments to strengthen the hypothesis. If the data do not support the hypothesis, then you should look for "human error" factors first. If these kinds of factors can be ruled out, suggest modifications to the hypothesis. You may also describe ways to test the new hypothesis. Ideally, scientists will thoroughly investigate a question until they are satisfied that they can explain the phenomenon of interest.

10. Share Findings with Other Scientists

The final phase of the scientific method is communicating your results to other scientists, either at scientific meetings or through a publication in a journal. When you submit a paper to refereed journals, it is read critically by other scientists in your field, and your methods, results, and conclusions are scrutinized. If any errors are discovered, they are corrected before your results are communicated to the scientific community at large.

Poster sessions are an excellent way to share preliminary findings with your colleagues. The emphasis in poster presentations is on the methods and the results. The informal atmosphere of most poster sessions promotes the exchange of ideas among scientists with common interests. See Chapter 7 on how to prepare a poster.

Oral presentations are different from both journal articles and poster sessions, because the speaker's delivery plays a critical role in the success of the communication. See Chapter 8 for tips on preparing and delivering an effective oral presentation.

Chapter 2

FINDING PRIMARY REFERENCES

The development of library research skills is an essential part of your training as a biology student. A vast body of literature is available on just about every topic. Efficiently finding exactly what you need requires practice and familiarity with library research tools.

In biology, sources are divided broadly into primary and secondary references. **Primary references** are the journal articles, dissertations, technical reports, or conference papers in which a scientist describes his or her original work. Primary references are written for fellow scientists—in other words, for a specialized audience. The objective of a primary reference is to present the essence of a scientist's work in a way that permits readers to duplicate the work for their own purposes and to refute or build on that work.

Secondary references include textbooks, review articles, and articles in popular magazines such as *Scientific American*. Secondary references are based on primary references, but they address a wider, less-specialized audience. In secondary references, there is less emphasis on the methodology and presentation of data. Results and their implications are described in general terms for the benefit of nonspecialist readers.

You will delve into the biological literature when you write laboratory reports, research papers, and other assignments. Although secondary references provide a good starting point for your work, it is important to be able to locate the primary sources on which the secondary sources are based. Only the primary literature provides you with a description of the methodology and the actual experimental results. With this information, you can draw your own conclusions from the author's data.

Although initially it is difficult to read primary literature, it becomes easier with practice, and your persistence will be rewarded with improved critical thinking skills. A further benefit of reading the primary literature is getting to know the scientists who work in a particular subdiscipline. You may discover that you are sufficiently interested in a subdiscipline to pursue graduate work with one or more of the authors of a journal article. Networking is as important in biology as in other fields.

How do you find primary references that are directly relevant to your topic? The fastest and easiest way is to search computer databases using keywords. Most university libraries have licensing agreements with the companies that produce the databases commonly used in biology. These licenses are almost always restrictive, making them available only to faculty, staff, and on-campus students. Thus, if you wish to research a particular topic using databases such as PubMed, BasicBIOSIS (FirstSearch), and the ISI Web of Science, you must be affiliated with a university or other organization that has such a licensing agreement.

Most of this chapter describes how to find primary references using databases. If you do not have access to these databases, however, you can still locate references the old-fashioned way. This method involves building a bibliography from sources cited in textbooks, journal articles, and other literature (see "References Cited," p. 13). This method is laborious and time-consuming because you are doing the physical work of the database, but the end result is often the same.

A disadvantage of using databases is that some older, seminal papers may not be indexed. If your assignment requires a thorough search of the literature, you will have to locate these older references the old-fashioned way.

Current Journal Articles

Check your campus library's website for electronic databases that you can search including: PubMed, Basic BIOSIS, ISI Web of Science. To find current journal articles in biology, use one of the following databases as a starting point.

- **PubMed.** PubMed is "a service of the U.S. National Library of Medicine <http://www.nlm.nih.gov/> that includes over 17 million citations from MEDLINE and other life science journals for biomedical articles back to the 1950s. PubMed includes links to full text articles and other related resources."

- **BasicBIOSIS (FirstSearch).** Database of articles from core popular and scholarly life science journals from the last five years.

- **ISI Web of Science.** Provides access to Science Citation Index Expanded (1955– present) and Social Sciences Citation Index (1956–present). Science Citation Index Expanded includes bibliographic information and abstracts found in 5700 major journals across 164 disciplines. Social Sciences Citation Index covers 1725 social sciences journals spanning 50 disciplines. Also provides a Cited Reference Search in both indexes that finds articles that have cited a previously published article.

Many of these databases provide the opportunity to download some articles as PDF (*portable document format*) files that can be viewed and printed through Adobe Acrobat Reader, which can be downloaded free of charge from http://www.adobe.com. If the articles are not available through a link, then access the journal directly through your library's ejournal pages. If you need to build a large bibliography on a specific topic very quickly, or if you want to search the literature both forward and backward in time, use the ISI Web of Science.

To Use Other Databases in FirstSearch (BasicBIOSIS) Depending on your topic, you may find some of the other FirstSearch databases helpful:

- MEDLINE (medicine and the health sciences)
- AGRICOLA (agriculture, forestry, animal science)
- GenSciIndex (general science, geology, and earth science)

Avoid databases that specialize in science magazine articles, because these articles are not considered to be primary references. Enter a keyword and examine the abstracts as before.

Electronic journals. Many scientific journals are available electronically. Check the library's website or ask the librarian if your library subscribes to any e-journals.

References Cited

Once you have found a highly relevant journal article, browse the References (Literature Cited) at the end of the article for other relevant journal articles. This kind of search is a very effective way to expand your bibliography, because it provides specific information on the topic of interest.

Books

Books may be primary or secondary references. Although books such as *Annual Reviews* are considered secondary references, the Literature Cited sections in review articles often are an excellent source of primary references.

The following steps are usually the ones to take when looking for books on a specific topic in an academic library:

1. Look for the Online Catalog on the library's home page.
2. Select **Search**.
3. Enter keyword(s). Be as specific as possible.
4. Book titles will be listed. Click on any titles that sound promising.
5. Write down the call number and note the availability of the book.
6. When you look for the book on the shelf, browse the titles of other books in the vicinity. Because the Library of Congress cataloging system groups books according to topic, you can often find additional sources shelved nearby.

The Internet

The Internet connects computers around the world. This connection allows you to communicate with other computer users on the network through e-mail, instant messages (IM), chat rooms, and the World Wide Web (www, or the Web).

Connecting to the Internet

To get on the Internet, you need a computer, an internet connection, an Internet service provider (ISP), and browsing software (such as Internet Explorer or Mozilla Firefox). If you are affiliated with a school, college, or library, the ISP is probably your organization's computer center; if you are making the connection from your home, you need a commercial ISP such as EarthLink or America Online.

Once you have set up an account with an ISP, you can use a browser to find information on the Internet. Sometimes your browser requires plug-ins (additional software) to work efficiently. Instructions for downloading and installing plug-ins are provided in the browser's message windows.

General Navigation

Figure 2.1 shows the menu bar and the toolbars for the most popular graphic browser, Microsoft Internet Explorer (IE). IE held more than 90%

Allows you to save your current search
location. In a future session, you merely
click the desired Favorite in the list to
return to its location.

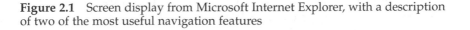

History lists the sites
that were recently visited.

Figure 2.1 Screen display from Microsoft Internet Explorer, with a description of two of the most useful navigation features

of the market share in desktop browsers in 2004, but critics say that IE has been slower than the other leading browser developers, Opera (<www.opera.com>) and Mozilla (<www.mozilla.org>), to improve security features such as pop-up blocking. Mozilla's browser looks similar to that of Netscape Navigator, a popular browser in the 1990s whose future is presently uncertain. You can run more than one browser on your computer, and the three leading browsers all support both Windows and Macintosh.

Browsers have navigation buttons, menus, and toolbars that you can use to search for information on the Internet. Some useful basic commands are described in Figure 2.1. A comprehensive explanation can be found in Harnack and Kleppinger (2001 and URLs contained therein).

Search Tools

Search tools (also called search engines) enable you to find information on specific topics by typing in keywords. The search tools scan millions of Internet documents for these keywords and then display a list of the documents (with links) in which these keywords appear.

Three useful search tools are Google (<http://www.google.com>), Google scholar (<http://www.scholar.google.com>), and SCIRUS (<http://www.scirus.com>). These index millions of Web pages and rank the search results according to the frequency of occurrence and relevance to the keywords. Metaengines such as Metacrawler (<http://www.go2net.com>) and Ask Jeeves! (<http://ask.com>) are also useful because they allow you to search several Web indexes simultaneously.

For more information on using search tools to find references, see Harnack and Kleppinger (2001).

Evaluate Internet Sources Critically

Although there is an incredible amount of information available on the Internet, much of this information may be unreliable. Whereas journal articles and books have undergone a rigorous review process, information on the Web may not have been checked by any authority other than the owner of the website.

Be particularly wary of companies and organizations who are more interested in trying to sell a product or an idea than in presenting factual information. The ending of the URL address may help you identify the sponsor, as shown in Table 2.1.

Websites are not considered primary references. When you write a laboratory report or research paper, make sure most of your references are part of the body of published literature, primarily journal articles. You may, however, supplement the literature cited with information retrieved from the Internet.

TABLE 2.1 Identifying sponsors of sites on the World Wide Web

TYPE OF WEB PAGE	PURPOSE	ENDING OF URL ADDRESS	EXAMPLES
Publically funded	To present information	.edu .gov	Colleges and universities USDA, CDC, NCBI
Business/ marketing	To sell a product	.com	Philip-Morris, Leica
Advocacy	To influence public opinion	.org	Republican Party, Wikipedia
News	To present very current information	.com	CNN, *USA Today*
Personal	To present information about an individual	Variety of endings, but has tilde (~) embedded in the URL	

Source: Modified from Widener University (<http://www.widener.edu/Tools_Resources/ Libraries/ Wolfgram_Memorial_Library/Evaluate_Web_Pages/659/?vobId=1816>) Accessed 2006 Aug 3.

Chapter 3

READING AND WRITING SCIENTIFIC PAPERS

No matter whether you are a student or are already engaged in a profession, writing is a fact of life. There are many reasons for writing: to express your feelings, to entertain, to communicate information, and to persuade. When you write scientific papers, your primary reason for writing is to clearly communicate information.

Types of Scientific Writing

Scientific writing takes many forms. As an undergraduate biology major, you will be asked to write laboratory reports, answer essay questions on exams, write summaries of journal articles, and do literature surveys on topics of interest. Upperclass students may write a research proposal for honors work, and then complete their project by submitting an honors thesis. Graduate students typically write master's theses and doctoral dissertations and defend their written work with oral presentations. Professors write lectures, letters of recommendation, grant proposals, articles, and reviews. In business and industry, scientific writing may take the form of progress reports, product descriptions, operating manuals, and sales and marketing material.

Hallmarks of Scientific Writing

What distinguishes scientific writing from other kinds of writing? One difference is the motive. Scientific writing aims to inform and expand our knowledge base rather than to entertain the reader. The reader is typically a fellow scientist who intends to use this information, for example, to learn more about a process or to improve a product.

A second difference is the style. A standard format, brevity, and proper use of grammar and punctuation are the hallmarks of well-written scientific papers. The authors have something important to communicate, and they want to make sure that others understand the significance of their work. Flowery language and "stream of consciousness" prose are not appropriate in scientific writing because they can obscure the writer's intended meaning.

A third difference between scientific and other types of writing is that scientific writing is factual and objective. The writer presents information without emotion and without editorializing.

Scientific Paper Format

Scientific papers are descriptions of how the scientific method was used to study a problem. They follow a standard format that allows the reader, first, to determine initial interest in the paper, second, to read a summary of the paper to learn more, and, finally, to read the paper itself for all the details. This format is very convenient, because it allows busy people to scan volumes of information in a relatively short time, then spend more time reading only those papers that truly provide the information they need.

Almost all scientific papers are organized as follows:

1. Title
2. List of Authors
3. Abstract
4. Introduction
5. Materials and Methods
6. Results
7. Discussion
8. References

1. The **Title** is a **short, informative description of the essence of the paper**. It should contain the fewest number of words that accurately convey the content. Readers use the title to determine their initial interest in the paper.

2. Only the names of **people who played an active role** in designing the experiment, carrying it out, and analyzing the data appear in the **List of Authors**.

3. The **Abstract** is a **summary of the entire paper** in 250 words or less. It contains an introduction (scope and purpose), a short description of the methods (one or two sentences about how the study was completed), results (the major findings of the study), and conclusions (implications of

the study). There are no literature citations or references to figures in the Abstract.

4. The **Introduction** concisely states what motivated the study, how it fits into the existing body of knowledge, and the objectives of the work. The Introduction consists of two primary parts:

a. **Background or historical perspective on the topic.** Primary journal articles and review articles, rather than other secondary sources such as textbooks and newspaper articles, are cited to provide the reader with direct access to the original work. Inconsistencies, unanswered questions, or new questions that resulted from previous work set the stage for the present study. An introduction usually progresses from general to specific and provides a rationale and context for the current study.

b. **Statement of objectives or hypotheses of the work.** What were the goals of the present study?

5. The **Materials and Methods** section describes, in full sentences and well-developed paragraphs, **how the experiment was done**. The author provides sufficient detail to allow another scientist to repeat the experiment. Volume, mass, concentration, growth conditions, temperature, pH, type of microscopy, statistical analyses, and sampling techniques are critical pieces of information that must be included. When and where the work was carried out is important if the study was done in the field (in nature), but is not included if the study was done in a laboratory. Conventional labware and laboratory techniques that are common knowledge (familiar to the audience) are not explained. In some instances, it is appropriate to use references to describe methods.

6. The **Results** section is **where the findings of the experiment are summarized**, without giving any explanations as to their significance (the "whys" are reserved for the Discussion section). A good Results section has two components:

- A *text*, which forms the body of this section
- Some form of *visual* that helps the reader comprehend the data and get the message faster than from reading a lengthy description

7. In the **Discussion** section, the **results are interpreted** and possible explanations are given. The author may:

- Summarize the results in a way that supports the conclusions
- Describe how the results relate to existing knowledge (literature sources)

- Describe inconsistencies in the data. This is preferable to concealing an anomalous result.

- Discuss possible sources of error

- Describe future extensions of the current work

8. **References** list the **outside sources** the authors consulted in preparing the paper. No one has time to return to a state of zero knowledge and rediscover known mechanisms and relationships. That is why scientists rely so heavily on information published by their colleagues. References are typically cited in the Introduction and Discussion sections of a scientific paper, and the procedures given in Materials and Methods are often modifications of those in previous work.

Styles for Documenting References

The Council of Science Editors (CSE Manual, 7th ed. 2006) recommends the following two formats for documenting references:

> **Citation-Sequence System**. In the *text*, the source of the cited information is provided in an abbreviated form as a number in square brackets or parentheses. On the *references pages* that follow the Discussion section, the sources are listed in **numerical order** and include the full reference.

> **Name-Year System**. In the *text*, the source is given in the form of author(s) and year. On the *references pages* that follow the Discussion section, the references are listed in **alphabetical order** according to the first author's last name.

The name-year system has the advantage that people working in the field will know the literature and, on seeing the authors' names, will understand the reference without having to check the reference list. This system is more commonly used and generally is preferred. With the citation-sequence system, for each reference the reader must turn to the reference list at the end of the paper to gain the same information.

Strategies for Reading Journal Articles

Papers in scientific journals are written by experts in the field. Because you are not yet an expert, you will probably find it difficult to read and understand journal articles. The following strategy may help.

Determine the topic. First, try to determine the topic of the article by reading the title and the abstract. Are the authors trying to answer a specific question, explain observations, present a theoretical model of a process, determine the relationship between one or more variables, or accomplish something else?

Acquire background information on the topic. Read about the topic in your textbook. Because textbook authors generally write for a student audience, not a group of experts, your textbook is likely to be easier to read. See "Strategies for Reading your Textbook" for some ways to read biology textbooks efficiently.

Read the Introduction. The introduction is usually easier to follow than the abstract. Skim the introduction with the following questions in mind:

- Why did the author(s) carry out this work?
- What are the main hypotheses?
- What was previously known about the topic or problem?
- What are the objectives of the current work?

Read the Results section selectively. Look at the figures and tables to determine what variables were studied. The independent variable (the one the investigator manipulated) is plotted on the x-axis, and the dependent variable(s) (the one that changes depending on the independent variable) is plotted on the y-axis. Also look for variables in column headings of tables.

There are two places to look for a qualitative description of each figure and table: the figure/table caption, and in the body of the Results section (text). The caption states the main idea of the visual. The topic sentence of the paragraph in the text does the same. Subsequent sentences in the paragraph provide details on what trends or findings the reader should notice in each visual. When you read about the results, ask yourself the following questions:

- What were the independent, dependent, and controlled variables?
- Was there a difference between the controls and the experimental groups?
- What were the main findings regarding the independent and dependent variables?

If necessary, reread the introduction to recall the main objectives and hypotheses of the work. Try to understand the big picture before concerning yourself with the details.

Read the Discussion section. The author typically presents his/her conclusions in this section and describes how the results of the study support these conclusions. This is where you can find out what was learned from the work. In particular:

- Were the hypotheses supported?
- What were the important findings?
- Were there any inconsistencies or unexpected results?
- What further work is necessary or already in progress?
- How does this paper relate to your own work?

Skim the Materials and Methods section. Scan the subheadings (if present) and the topic sentence of each paragraph to identify the basic approach. Do not be concerned with the details at this stage.

Read the article several times. Even experts must read journal articles several times before they understand the methodology and the implications of the findings. It is wise to take notes the first time you read the article, noting what is confusing. Consult your notes when you read the article again, and try to clarify what you didn't understand the first time through. Each time you read the article, you will understand a little more.

Strategies for Reading your Textbook

The following strategies are based on the proposition that you cannot read a chapter in a biology textbook just once and understand it completely. Repetition is a key ingredient in learning the material. Repetition not only provides you with multiple opportunities to be exposed to the material, but also gives you time to digest it. The basic approach is to read for organization and key concepts first, and then to fill in the details with each subsequent reading.

The two strategies described here work best with a chapter or section of text no longer than 25–30 pages. The first strategy is proposed by Counselling Services at the University of Victoria, Canada (Palmer-Stone, 2001).

1. Take no more than 25 minutes to:
   - Read the chapter title, introduction, and summary (at the end of the chapter, if present)
   - Read the headings and subheadings
   - Read the chapter title, introduction, summary, headings, and subheadings again
   - Skim the topic sentence of each paragraph (usually the first or second sentence)
   - Skim italicized or boldfaced words

2. Close your textbook. Take a full 30 minutes to:
   - Write down everything you can remember about what you read in the chapter (make a "mind map"). Each time you come to a dead end, use memory techniques such as associating ideas from your reading to lecture notes or other life experiences; visualizing pages, pictures, or graphs; staring out the window to daydream; letting your mind go blank.
   - Figure out how all this material is related. Organize it according to what makes sense in your mind, not necessarily according to how it is organized in the textbook. Write down questions and possible contradictions to check on later.

3. Open your textbook. Fill in the blanks in your mind map with a different colored pencil.

4. Read the chapter again, this time normally. Make another mind map.

A second strategy is:

1. Skim the chapter title, headings, and subheadings for an overview of the chapter content. Write down the headings and subheadings in the form of an outline.

2. Look at your outline and ask yourself the following questions:
   - What is the main topic of this chapter?
   - How do each of the headings relate to the topic?
   - How does each subheading relate to its heading?

3. Read each section, paying special attention to the topic sentence of each paragraph. At the end of each section, summarize the content in your own words. Answer the following questions:
   - What's the point?
   - What do I understand?
   - What is confusing?

4. If you read the assigned pages before the lecture, you can pay attention to the lecture content instead of just frantically taking notes. Check to see if there is a lecture notebook that accompanies your textbook. The lecture notebook contains the figures in black and white, and allows you to take notes during lecture directly on the figures.

5. After the lecture, while the information is still fresh in your mind, reread your notes on your reading. Ask yourself
   - What topics did the instructor emphasize in lecture? Fill in your lecture notes with details from your textbook.
   - What material do I understand better now?
   - What questions remain?

6. Remember that each time you read the material, you will learn a little more.

Study Groups

If you have read the material several times, taken notes, and listened attentively in lecture, but still have questions, talk about the material with your classmates. Small study groups are one reason why students who choose to major in the sciences persist in the sciences, rather than switching to a non-science major (Light, 2001).

What are some benefits of participating in small study groups? One benefit is the comfort level. You may be more likely to talk about problems when you are among your peers; after all, they are not the ones who assign your grade. Secondly, when a group is composed of peers with a similar knowledge base, group members speak the same language. Your instructor speaks a different language, because he or she has already struggled to master the material. When you communicate with your classmates, you verbalize your ideas at a level that is appropriate for your audience of peers. Collaborative learning reflects the way scientists exchange information and share findings in the real world. A spirit of camaraderie develops when people work together toward a common goal. The prospect of learning difficult subject matter is no longer so daunting when you have support from a small group of like-minded individuals. The hard work may even be fun when there is good group social chemistry. Finally, the most important aspect of participating in a study group is the opportunity to teach others what you have learned. However, **group study is not a substitute for studying alone**. You must hold yourself accountable for reading the material, taking notes, and figuring out what you do not understand before you meet with your group. If you have not struggled to understand the material yourself, you are not in a position to help a classmate.

DO NOT PLAGIARIZE: Paraphrase and Cite What You Read

One of the best ways to know whether or not you understand an author's work is to summarize the key findings in your own words. Do not make the mistake of simply copying the text word for word from the textbook or journal article, just because you think that you could not have said it better yourself. Get into the habit of paraphrasing the information in the source document, and carefully noting the source (see "Documenting Sources" in Chapter 4). By convention, **direct quotations are not used in scientific writing**.

Plagiarism is taking someone else's ideas and passing them off as your own. This includes citing the source but still copying the words verbatim. Usually plagiarism is unintentional and is the result of not having a clear understanding of the material. If you can state in your own words what you think the author meant, then you probably understood it. If not, you may have to read the paper a few more times or ask for help from your instructor or a fellow student.

To avoid plagiarism when taking notes, follow this collective advice of Lannon (2000), McMillan (1997), Pechenik (2004), and other authorities on scientific writing:

- Don't take notes until you have read the source text at least twice. You have to understand it before you can summarize it.
- Retain key words.
- Use your own words and write in your own style.
- Distinguish your own ideas and questions from those of the source text (e.g., "Me: Confusing!").
- Don't cite out of context. Preserve the author's original meaning.
- Fully document the source for later listing under References.

The Benefits of Learning to Write Scientific Papers

Why is it valuable to learn how to write scientific papers? First, scientific writing is a systematic approach to describing a problem. By writing what you know (and what you do not know) about the problem, it is often possible to identify gaps in your own knowledge.

Secondly, scientific writing aims to persuade the reader of the validity of the procedures, results, and conclusions described in the paper. Improving your reasoning abilities in laboratory reports may have a positive effect on other areas of your life as well.

Third, when you learn to write lab reports, you are investing in your future. Publications in the sciences are affirmation from your colleagues that your work has merit; you have been accepted into the community of experts in your field. Even if your career path is not in the sciences, scientific writing is very logical and organized, characteristics appreciated by everyone.

Credibility and Reputation

The credibility and reputation of scientists are established primarily by their ability to communicate effectively through their written reports.

Poorly written papers, regardless of the importance of the content, may not get published if the reviewers do not understand what the writer intended to say.

You should think about your reputation even as a student. When you write your laboratory reports in an accepted, concise, and accurate manner, your instructor knows that you are serious about your work. Your instructor appreciates not only the time and effort required to understand the subject matter, but also your willingness to write according to the standards of the profession.

Model Papers

Before writing your first laboratory report, go to the library and take a look at some biology journals such as *American Journal of Botany, Ecology, The EMBO Journal, Journal of Biological Chemistry, Journal of Molecular Biology,* and *Marine Biology.* Photocopy one or two journal articles that interest you so you can refer to them for format questions.

Almost all journals devote one page or more to "Instructions to Authors," in which specific information is conveyed regarding length of the manuscript, general format, figures, conventions, references, and so on. Skim this section to get an idea of what journal editors expect from scientists who wish to have their work published.

Because most beginning biology students find journal articles hard to read, a sample student laboratory report is given in Chapter 6. Read the comments in the left margin as you peruse the report to familiarize yourself with the basics of scientific paper format and content, as well as purpose, audience, and tone.

Chapter 4

Step-by-Step Instructions for Preparing a Laboratory Report or Scientific Paper

In order to prepare a well-written laboratory report according to accepted conventions, the following skills are required:

- A solid command of the English language
- An understanding of the scientific method
- An understanding of scientific concepts and terminology
- Advanced word processing skills
- Knowledge of computer graphing software
- The ability to read and evaluate journal articles
- The ability to search the primary literature efficiently
- The ability to evaluate the reliability of Internet sources.

If you are a first- or second-year college student, it is unlikely that you possess all of these skills when you are asked to write your first laboratory report. Don't worry. The instructions in this chapter will guide you through the steps involved in preparing the first draft of a laboratory report. Revision is addressed in the next chapter, and the Appendices will help you with word processing and graphing tasks. Most campuses have a writing center that you can go to for help. It is highly recommended that you visit the writing center at least once before you hand in your first written assignment.

Timetable

Preparing a laboratory report or scientific paper is hard work. It will take much more time than you expect. Writing the first draft is only the first

TABLE 4.1 Timetable for writing your laboratory report

TIME FRAME	ACTIVITY	RATIONALE
Day 1	Complete laboratory exercise.	It's fun. Besides, you need data to write about.
Days 2–3	Write first draft of laboratory report.	The lab is still fresh in your mind. You also need time to complete the subsequent tasks before the due date.
Day 4	Proofread and revise first draft (hard copy).	Always take a break after writing the first draft and before revising it. This "distance" gives you objectivity to read your paper critically.
Day 5	Give first draft to a peer for review or go to the writing center.	Your peer reviewer is a sounding board for your writing. He/she will give you feedback on whether what you intended to write actually comes across in the text. You may wish to alert your peer reviewer to concerns you have about your paper (see "Look at the Big Picture" in Chapter 5). *A note of caution*: **be careful not to share your documents with classmates. If your work is copied by another student, Stony Brook considers you an accomplice to academic dishonesty.**
	Arrange to meet with your reviewer after he/she has had time to review your paper ("writing conference").	An informal discussion is useful for providing immediate exchange of ideas and concerns.

step. You must also allow time for proofreading and revision. If you work on your paper in stages, the final product will be much better than if you try to do everything at the last minute.

The timetable outlined in Table 4.1 breaks the writing process down into stages, based on a one-week time frame. You can adjust the time frame according to your own deadlines.

Format Your Report Correctly

Although content is important, the appearance of your paper is what makes the first impression on the reader. If the pages are out of order and the ink is faded, subconsciously or not, the reader is going to associate a

TABLE 4.1 *Continued*

TIME FRAME	ACTIVITY	RATIONALE
Day 6	Peer reviewer reviews laboratory report.	The peer reviewer should review the paper according to two sets of criteria. One is the conventions of scientific writing as described in "Scientific Paper Format," and the other is the set of questions in "Get Feedback" in Chapter 5.
	Hold writing conference during which the reviewer returns the first draft to the writer.	An informal discussion between the writer and the reviewer is useful to give the writer an opportunity to explain what he/she intended to accomplish, and for the reviewer to provide feedback.
Days 6–7	Revise laboratory report.	Based on your discussion with your reviewer, revise as necessary. Remember that you do not have to accept all of the reviewer's suggestions.
Day 8	Hand in final copy to instructor.	Your instructor wants to know what you've learned (we never stop learning either!).

sloppy paper with sloppy science. You cannot afford that kind of reputation. In order for your work to be taken seriously, your paper has to have a professional appearance.

Scientific journals specify the format in their "Instructions to Authors" section. If your instructor has not given you specific instructions, the layout specified in Table 4.2 will give your paper a professional look.

Consult the sample "good" student laboratory report in Chapter 6 for an overview of the style and layout. An electronic file called "Biology Lab Report Template," available at <www.sinauer.com/Knisely/> is formatted according to the guidelines of Table 4.2 and provides prompts that help you get started writing in scientific paper format. For details on how to format documents in Microsoft Word, see "Formatting a Document" in Appendix 1.

Computer Savvy

Know your PC and your word processing software. Most of the tasks you will encounter in writing your laboratory report are described in Appendix 1 "Word Processing Basics in Microsoft Word 2007" and Appendix 2 "Data

TABLE 4.2 Instructions to authors of laboratory reports

FEATURE	LAYOUT
Paper	8½" x 11" (or DIN A4) white bond, double-sided if possible
Margins	1" all around
Font size	12 pt (points to the inch)
Typeface	Times Roman or another *serif* font. A serif is a small stroke that embellishes the character at the top and bottom. The serifs create a strong horizontal emphasis, which helps the eye scan lines of text more easily.
Symbols	Use word processing software. Do not write symbols in by hand.
Pagination	Arabic number, bottom of each page except the first
Justification	Align left/ragged right or Full/even edges
Spacing	Double
New paragraph	Indent 0.5"
Title page	Title, authors (your name first, lab partner second), name of instructor, class, and date
Headings	Align headings for Abstract, Introduction, Materials and Methods, Results, Discussion, and References on left margin. Use consistent format for capitalization. Do not start each section on a new page unless it works out that way coincidentally.
Subheadings	Use sparingly and maintain consistent format.
Tables and figures	Incorporate into text as close as possible after the paragraph where they are first mentioned. Use descriptive titles, sequential numbering, proper position above or below visual.
Sketches	Hand-drawn in pencil or ink. Other specifications as in "Tables and figures," above.
References	Name-Year System: List references in alphabetical order by the first author's last name. Use a hanging indent (all lines but the first indented) to separate individual references. Use accepted punctuation and format.
Assembly	Place pages in order, staple top left.

Management in Microsoft Excel." If there is a task that is not covered in these appendices, write it down and ask an expert later. If you run into a major problem that prevents you from using your PC, you should have a backup plan in place (familiarity with another PC).

Always back up your files. Save your file frequently while writing your paper. Set up your computer to automatically save data every 10 minutes, so that in the event of a power failure you will have lost only 10 minutes' worth of work. These tasks are described in Appendix 1. In addition, save a backup copy on a USB jump drive, CD, DVD, or external hard drive in the event of an internal hard drive failure.

Install antivirus software on your computer, and always check disks and CDs for viruses before you use them. Beware of files attached to e-mail messages. Do not open attachments unless you are sure they come from a reliable source.

Store CDs and DVDs in protective boxes. Keep hard drives and USB flash drives away from magnetic devices (TV, speakers, etc.) and excess humidity, heat, and cold.

Getting Started

Set aside 1 hour to begin writing the laboratory report as soon as possible after doing the laboratory exercise. Restricting the time to 1 hour forces you to make effective use of limited time. It also takes advantage of the attention span to which you are accustomed in lecture.

If your paper is progressing well and you are having fun, extend the 1-hour period until you perceive a loss of concentration. Promise yourself a reward after a certain amount of progress. It is not necessary to deprive yourself of pleasure as long as you work efficiently.

Reread the Laboratory Exercise

You cannot begin to write a paper without a sense of purpose. What were the objectives of your experiment? What questions are you supposed to answer? Take notes on the laboratory exercise to prevent problems with plagiarism when you write your laboratory report.

Audience and Tone

Scientific papers are written for scientists. Similarly, laboratory reports are intended to describe procedures and findings to fellow students. Of course, your instructor is going to read and evaluate your laboratory report, but your instructor is not the audience for whom you are writing. You are *writing for your peers*—students just like yourself.

Write as though your peers are fellow scientists, not students in a classroom situation. Note the difference between the original text and the revision in the following examples:

> **EXAMPLE 1:** The experiments performed by the students dealt with how different wavelengths of light affect seed germination.

> **REVISION:** The purpose of the experiment was to determine how different wavelengths of light affect seed germination.

> **EXAMPLE 2:** The purpose of this experiment is to become acquainted with new lab techniques such as protein analysis, serial dilutions, and use of the spectrophotometer.

> **REVISION:** The purpose of this experiment was to use the Biuret assay to determine protein concentration in egg white.

Your audience has a knowledge base similar to your own. Thus, when you introduce your topic and describe and interpret your results, you should assume that your audience will know some scientific vocabulary, but you should clarify or define less familiar terms. When deciding on how much background information to include, assume that your audience knows what you learned in class.

Keep the tone of your laboratory report factual and objective. Do not use jargon (terms known only to experts) or copy information verbatim from journal articles or your textbook. Remember that your objective is to write for your peers in a style that they can understand clearly.

Start with the Materials and Methods Section

The order in which you write the different sections is not the order in which they appear in the finished laboratory report. The rationale for this plan will become obvious as you read on. The Materials and Methods section requires the least amount of thought, because you are primarily restating the procedure in your own words.

Writing Style

Laboratory *exercises* are typically written in present tense, often with instructions in the form of a numbered list. When you write your laboratory *report*, however, summarize what you did in **full sentences and well-developed paragraphs**. Use **past tense**, because you completed the experiment some time ago.

You will have to make decisions on verb voice when you describe the procedure. For example:

ACTIVE VOICE: I peeled and homogenized the potatoes.

PASSIVE VOICE: The potatoes were peeled and homogenized.

The sentence written in active voice is more natural and dynamic, but it shifts the emphasis from the subject, "the potatoes" to "I." When you describe a procedure, *who* did it is not as important as *what* was done. Passive voice places the emphasis on the potatoes, where it belongs. Take care not to overuse passive voice, however, because it can make your writing seem stuffy and impersonal. See the section "Active and Passive Voice" in Chapter 5 for appropriate use of active and passive voice.

Details: To Include or Not To Include?

When you first begin to write scientific papers, it may be hard to decide how much detail to include in the Materials and Methods section. On the one hand, too many details bore the reader; on the other hand, you must include enough information to allow the reader to repeat the experiment. The following are some examples of things to avoid and include in Materials and Methods sections.

Avoid listing materials. The separation of the heading "Materials and Methods" into two parts is understandably confusing for beginning students. The implication is that the materials should be listed separately from the methods. In fact, **materials should not be listed separately** unless the strain of bacteria, vector (plasmid), growth media, or chemicals were obtained from a special or noncommercial source. It will be obvious to the reader what materials are required on reading the methods.

Avoid any reference to the container. Consider the following example:

EXAMPLE: Eight clean beakers were labeled with the following concentrations of hydrogen peroxide and those solutions were created and placed in the appropriate beaker: 0, 0.1, 0.2, 0.5, 0.8, 1.0, 5.0, and 10.0.

There are two problems with this passage: (1) It is not necessary to mention that clean, suitable containers were used to store the solutions; this is common practice in the laboratory. (2) The contents are more important than the label and the appropriate units must be mentioned.

> REVISION: The following hydrogen peroxide solutions were
> prepared: 0, 0.1, 0.2, 0.5, 0.8, 1.0, 5.0, and 10.0%.

Avoid lengthy descriptions of routine procedures. Your peers have learned certain basic laboratory techniques, such as using an electronic balance to weigh chemicals, a vortex mixer to mix solutions, a spectrophotometer to measure absorbance (optical density) of solutions, and micropipettors to measure small volumes. The amount of detail in the following examples is therefore unnecessary.

> EXAMPLE: To make the dilution, a micropipettor was used
> to release 45, 90, 135, and 180 µL of bovine
> serum albumin (BSA) into four different test
> tubes. To complete the dilution, 255, 210, 165,
> and 120 µL of TBS was added, respectively.

> REVISION: The following concentrations of BSA were pre-
> pared for the Bradford assay: 300, 600, 900, and
> 1200 µg/mL.

With appropriate instruction, making dilutions of stock solutions becomes a routine procedure. In the above example, you should assume that your peers can make the solution using the appropriate measuring instruments *as long as you specify the final concentration*.

> EXAMPLE: The test tubes were carried over to the spec-
> trophotometer and the wavelength was set to
> 595 nm (nanometer). The spectrophotometer
> was zeroed using the blank. Each of the remain-
> ing 8 samples in the test tubes were individual-
> ly placed into the empty spec tube, which was
> then placed in the spectrophotometer where the
> absorbance was determined.

> REVISION: The absorbance of each sample was measured
> with a spectrophotometer at 595 nm.

However, if you have made an alteration to a standard or otherwise routine procedure, then you must state those detailed changes.

Avoid giving "previews" of your data analysis in the Materials and Methods section. Consider the following passage:

> **EXAMPLE:** A graph was plotted with Absorbance on the *y*-axis and Protein concentration on the *x*-axis. An equation was found to fit the line, then the unknown protein absorbances that fell on the graph were plugged into the equation, and a concentration was found.

> **REVISION:** *Delete this entire passage.*

Making graphs is something that you do when you summarize your raw data, but it is not part of the experimental procedure. How and why you chose to organize the data will become obvious to the reader in the Results section, where you display graphs, tables, and other visuals and describe the noteworthy findings. State how your data was collected and analyzed as necessary for the reader to understand or repeat your work. For example, you might state that *P*-values were determined by using the Chitest function of MSExcel.

Include all relevant information needed to repeat the experiment. Consider the following example:

> **EXAMPLE:** In this lab, we mixed varying amounts of BSA stock solution with varying amounts of TBS using a vortex mixer. We used a spectrophotometer to measure absorbance of the 4 BSA samples, and then we determined the concentration of 4 dilutions of egg white from the standard curve.

This procedure does not give the reader enough information to repeat the experiment, because essential details like *what concentrations of BSA* were used to construct the standard curve, *what dilutions of egg white* were tested, and the *wavelength* set on the spectrophotometer are left out.

> **REVISION:** BSA solutions (2, 3, 5, 10 mg/mL) were prepared in Tris-buffered saline (TBS). The egg white sample was serially diluted 1/5, 1/15, 1/60, and 1/300 with TBS. The absorbance of all samples was measured at 550 nm using a Spec 20 spectrophotometer.

Cite published sources. If you are paraphrasing a published laboratory exercise, it is necessary to cite the source (see "Documenting Sources").

Do the Results Section Next

The Results section is a *summary* of the key findings of your experiment. This section has two components:

- Visuals, such as tables and figures
- A body, or text, in which you describe the findings presented in the visuals.

Describe the findings in an objective manner, without explaining why or discussing possible implications.

When you work on the Results section, you will complete the following tasks, which are often done concurrently, not necessarily sequentially:

- **Analyze the raw data.** Raw data are all the observations and measurements that you recorded in your lab notebook. It is your job as the author to analyze all these data and process the information for the reader. **Do not simply transfer raw data into your lab report** (your instructor may ask you to attach pages from your lab notebook as an appendix, however). Instead, summarize the data by eliminating aberrant results (only if you realized that you made a mistake in obtaining these results), averaging replicates, using statistical methods to see possible trends, and/or selecting representative pictures (micrographs or digital images). The goal of data analysis in general is to try to figure out what the data show; more specifically, you are interested in whether the data support or negate your hypotheses.

- **Organize summarized data in tables or figures.** When you organize summarized data in a table or plot numerical values on a graph, you may be able to see trends that were not apparent before. Effective visuals are more powerful than words alone and they provide strong support for your arguments. See "Organizing Your Data."

- **Decide in which order to present the tables and figures.** The sequence should be logical, so that the first visual provides a basis for the next or so that the reader can easily follow your line of reasoning.

- **Describe each visual in turn and refer to it parenthetically.** You should first describe what you want the reader to notice about the visual. Refer to the visual by number in parentheses at the end of the first sentence in which you describe it. Position the visual after the descriptive paragraph (Figure 4.1). Other examples of good descriptions of visuals are given in Figures 4.2 and 4.5.

Tips for Writing the Body of the Results Section

Specify the visual that contains the data that you are describing. Refer to Figure 4.1 as you read the following passage:

EXAMPLE: The results that were obtained while completing the lab clearly showed that the percentage of male gametophytes increased with population density initially, but above 75 gametophytes/plate, the percentage of males leveled out at about 72%.

Figure 4.1 Excerpt from a Results section showing a properly formatted figure with one line (data set); text that describes the figure precedes it.

This passage is unsuitable because we don't know where to find the results the author is describing. Always refer to the visual parenthetically so that the reader can look at the visual presentation of the data while reading the author's description of those data.

> **REVISION:** The percentage of male gametophytes increased with population density initially, but above 75 gametophytes/plate, the percentage of males leveled out at about 72% (Figure 1).

Eliminate unnecessary introductions. Look at Figure 4.2 as you read the following example:

> **EXAMPLE:** Table 1 shows the effects of light and hormones on the germination of light-sensitive lettuce seeds. One group of seeds was treated with ABA and left under a fluorescent light, while another group received GA in the dark. It can be seen that the majority of the seeds (92.5%) germinated in the light, but fewer germinated in the light when ABA was present.

The first sentence of this passage is unnecessary, because **it says nothing substantive about the data contained in Table 1**; instead, it describes the layout of the table, which needs no description. The second sentence is also unnecessary, because it restates the materials and methods, but says nothing about the results. The first part of the third sentence ("It can be seen that") is simply verbiage.

Avoid other unnecessary introductions such as:

- It was found that…
- When the test plates were observed and counted, …
- There is also a general trend where…
- It can be determined that…
- Table 1 shows that there is a relationship between hormones and seed germination. (*What* is the relationship?)

Scientific writing is concise and to the point. When you write the body of the Results section, eliminate unnecessary introductions. Instead, jump right in with a substantive observation. Write in past tense, because in scientific writing, present tense denotes that the statement is a generally accepted fact (see "Present Tense or Past Tense?" in Chapter 5). It remains to be seen if your results are accepted by the scientific community!

Text describing the table immediately precedes the table. Skip a line before and after the table.

Abscisic acid (ABA) and gibberellic acid (GA) had opposite effects on seed germination (Table 1). The majority of the seeds (92.5%) germinated in the light, but fewer germinated when they were exposed to 0.05-8 µM ABA. On the other hand, only 25% of the seeds germinated in the dark. This percentage increased when the seeds were exposed to 10-40 µM GA.

Refer to the table number parenthetically

Arabic number

Table caption is positioned above table; consists of Arabic number and title in a smaller font (10).

1 space   2 spaces (not colon or period)

Descriptive title; not a complete sentence. Essence of table can be understood without referring to the body of the Results section.

Table 1 Interaction between light and hormones in the germination of light-sensitive lettuce seeds

First word of column heading is generally capitalized (except for words such as pH and cDNA that begin with a lower case letter)

Column headings include units in parentheses where appropriate

Light treatment	ABA (µM)	GA (µM)	Seed germination (%)
White fluorescent light	0		92.5
	0.05		15
	2		8
	8		0
Dark		0	25
		10	42
		20	63
		40	37

Categories (dependent variables) are arranged in columns, not rows

Horizontal lines are used sparingly

No vertical lines are used

Figure 4.2   Excerpt from a Results section showing a properly formatted table preceded by the text that describes the data in the table

REVISION: The majority of the seeds (92.5%) germinated in the light, but fewer seeds germinated when they were exposed to 0.05-8 µM ABA (Table 1).

Visuals

The most common visuals in scientific writing are tables and figures. A **table** is defined by Webster's dictionary as "a systematic arrangement of data usually in rows and columns for ready reference." A **figure** is any visual that is not a table. Thus, line graphs, bar graphs, pie graphs, drawings, gel photos, X-ray images, and microscope images are all called *figures* in scientific papers.

Do not feel that you have to have visuals in your lab report. If you can state the results in a sentence, then **no visual** is needed (see "Organizing Your Data," Example 1, p. 47).

Tables. Tables are used to display large quantities of numbers and other information that would be tedious to read in prose such as summary data or statistical results (Figure 4.3). Arrange the categories vertically, rather than horizontally, as this arrangement is easier for the reader to follow (see, for example, Table 1 in Figure 4.2). List the items in a logical order (e.g., sequential, alphabetical, or increasing or decreasing value). Include the units in each column heading to save yourself the trouble of writing the units after each number entry in the table.

By convention, tables in scientific papers do not have vertical lines to separate the columns, and horizontal lines are used only to separate the table caption from the column headings, the headings from the data, and the data from any footnotes.

Give each table a caption that includes a number and a title. Center the caption or align it on the left margin *above* the table. Use Arabic numbers, and number the tables consecutively in the order they are discussed in the text. Notice that in this book, the table and figure numbers are pre-

Table 1   Chi-Square Analyses of Monohybrid and Dihybrid Corn Crosses

		Group (n = 160)		Class (n = 960)	
Parental cross	df	χ^2	P	χ^2	P
Monohybrid					
R/R x r/r	1	1.060	0.300	0.020	0.890
Su/Su x su/su	1	0.067	0.796	0.024	0.877
Dihybrid					
R/R Su/Su x r/r su/su	3	4.700	0.195	2.988*	0.393*

Note: *this group only counted 832 kernels from the dihybrid cross.

Figure 4.3   Example of a table that summarizes statistical analyses.

ceded by the chapter number. This system helps orient the reader in long manuscripts, but is not necessary in short papers like your laboratory report.

Titles consist of a precise noun phrase, not a complete sentence, and only the first word and proper nouns are capitalized. The reader should be able to understand the essence of the table without having to refer to the body (the text) of the Results section.

> FAULTY: Table 1 Table of interaction between light and hormones in the germination of light-sensitive lettuce seeds [Do not start a title for a visual with a description of the visual.]

> FAULTY: Table 1 Seed germination data [Do not write vague and undescriptive titles.]

> REVISION: Table 1 Interaction between light and hormones in the germination of light-sensitive lettuce seeds

A table is always positioned *after* the text in which you refer to it (see Figure 4.2). Mention the table number in parentheses at the end of the first sentence in which you describe the table contents. That way the reader can refer to the table as you describe what you consider to be important.

In your laboratory report, it is not necessary to include a table when you already have a graph that shows the same data. Make *either* a table *or* a graph—not both—to present a given data set.

Tables can be constructed in either Microsoft Word (see Appendix 1, Section 2.12) or Microsoft Excel (see Appendix 2, Section 2.1).

Line graphs. Line graphs (or XY graphs) are perhaps the most frequently used type of graph in biology. Line graphs are used to display a trend or an important relationship between one or more variables. The data displayed in line graphs are **continuous and numerical**.

By convention, the independent variable (the one the scientist manipulates) is plotted on the x-axis, and the dependent variable (the one that changes in response to the independent variable) is plotted on the y-axis. The data then show the effect of x on y, or y as a function of x.

There are a number of formats for plotting data on an XY graph (Figure 4.4). Situations in which each format might be used are given.

Figures are always numbered and titled *beneath* the visual (see Figures 4.1 and 4.5). The captions may be centered or placed flush on the left mar-

A

Format: Data points, no connecting line

Uses: As a preliminary display before deciding on a better alternative; to emphasize variability in the data

B

Format: Data points connected by a smoothed or straight line

Uses: To describe the physical phenomena represented by a few data points; contains an element of prediction of what happens between the data points.

Figure 4.4 Different formats for XY graphs

gin of the report. Arabic numbers are used, and the figures are numbered consecutively in the order they are discussed in the text.

Figure titles should consist of a precise noun phrase, not a complete sentence, and only the first word and proper nouns are capitalized. The reader should be able to understand the title without referring to the text in the Results section.

FAULTY: Figure 1 Percentage of male gametophytes vs. population density [Do not restate the y-axis label versus the x-axis label as the figure title.]

FAULTY: Figure 1 shows the effect of population density on the percentage of male gametophytes in wild type *Ceratopteris* [Separate the figure number and the title.]

FAULTY: Figure 1 Line graph of the effect of population density on the percentage of male gametophytes in wild type *Ceratopteris* [Do not start a title for a visual with a description of the visual.]

C   **Label (units)**

Format: Line without data points

Uses: Never use this format to present experimental data, because the actual data are not shown. This format might be used to present model data or predictions.

D   **Label (units)**

Format: Data points connected by a trendline

Uses: (1) To determine if there is a correlation between two variables; (2) To predict one variable when the other is known (e.g., standard curve)

Figure 4.4 *Continued*

FAULTY: Figure 1 Averaged class data for C-fern experiment [Do not write vague and undescriptive titles.]

REVISION: Figure 1 Effect of population density on the percentage of male gametophytes in wild type *Ceratopteris*

If there is more than one data set (line) on the figure, you have three options:

- Add a brief label (no border, no arrows) next to each line
- Use a different symbol for each line and label the symbols in a key (as in Figure 4.5). Place the key without a border within the axes of the graph. This is the easiest option if you are using Excel to plot your data.
- If the first two options make the figure look cluttered, identify the symbols in the figure caption.

All three formats are acceptable in scientific papers as long as you use them consistently.

Figures in your laboratory report should be prepared according to the guidelines specified by the Council of Science Editors (CSE Manual, 2006). Although you may wish to plot a rough draft of your graphs by

The percentage of male gametophytes increased with population density of the wild type strain, but there were no male gametophytes at any density in the Her 1 strain (Figure 2).

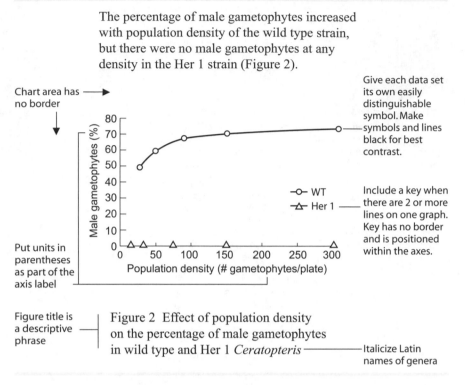

Chart area has no border

Give each data set its own easily distinguishable symbol. Make symbols and lines black for best contrast.

Include a key when there are 2 or more lines on one graph. Key has no border and is positioned within the axes.

Put units in parentheses as part of the axis label

Figure title is a descriptive phrase

Figure 2 Effect of population density on the percentage of male gametophytes in wild type and Her 1 *Ceratopteris*

Italicize Latin names of genera

Figure 4.5 Excerpt from a Results section showing a properly formatted figure with two sets of data. A legend (key) is needed to distinguish the two lines. The text that describes the figure precedes it.

hand, you must learn how to use computer plotting software to make graphs. Microsoft Excel is a plotting program for novices, (see Appendix 2) and it is readily available and fairly easy to use. The time you invest now in learning to plot data on the computer will be invaluable in your upper-level courses and later in your career.

Bar graphs. A bar graph allows you to compare individual sets of data when these data are **non-numerical or discontinuous**—this is the main difference between line graphs and bar graphs. For example, if you wanted to compare the final height of the same species of plant treated with four different nutrient solutions (Figure 4.6), each bar could be used to represent the plants treated with one nutrient solution. The data plotted on the *x*-axis are non-numerical, because different nutrient solutions (not numbers) are being compared. The data are discontinuous, because the

Figure 1 Final height of corn plants after 4-week treatment with different nutrient solutions.

Figure 4.6 This figure is an example of a column graph.

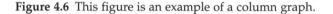

individual solutions have no effect on the growth of the plants treated with the other nutrient solutions.

Bar graphs can be arranged either vertically (Figure 4.6, also called a column graph) or horizontally (Figure 4.7). The arrangement you use

Figure 1 Final height of corn plants after 4-week treatment with different nutrient solutions.

Figure 4.7 This figure is an example of a horizontal bar graph.

Figure 1 Difference in height of groups of light-grown and dark-grown bean seedlings at 5, 10, and 15 days after planting.

Figure 4.8 This figure is an example of a clustered bar graph. Each bar in the cluster must be easily distinguishable from its neighbor.

often depends on your sub-discipline, but the horizontal arrangement is more practical when the category labels are long.

The bars should be placed sequentially, but if there is no particular order, then put the control treatment bar far left in column graphs or at the top in horizontal bar graphs. Order the experimental treatment bars from shortest to longest (or vice versa) to facilitate comparison among the different conditions. The baseline does not have to be visible, but all the bars must be aligned as if there were a baseline.

The bars should always be wider than the spaces between them. In a graph with clustered bars, make sure each bar has sufficient contrast so that it can be distinguished from its neighbor (Figure 4.8).

Pie graphs. A pie graph is used to show data as a percentage of the total data. For example, if you were doing a survey of insects found in your backyard, a pie graph would be effective in showing the percentage of each kind of insect out of all the insects sampled (Figure 4.9). There should be between 2 and 8 segments in the pie. Place the largest segment in the right-hand quadrant with the segments decreasing in size clockwise. Combine small segments under the heading "Other." Position labels and percentages horizontally outside of the segments for easy reference.

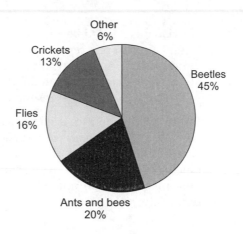

Figure 1   Composition of insects in backyard survey.

Figure 4.9 Pie graphs are used to show data as a percentage of the total data.

Organizing Your Data

Reread the questions in the laboratory exercise to determine what your instructor expects you to learn from the data. You may also find specific instructions on how to organize the data (tables, line graphs, bar graphs, etc.). Based on these expectations, decide which visual is best. Ask yourself the following questions:

- Can I state the results in one sentence? If so, then **no visual** is needed.
- Are the numbers themselves more important than the trend shown by the numbers? If so, then use a **table**.
- Is the trend more important than the numbers themselves? If so, use a **graph**.

The following examples demonstrate that there may be more than one good way to organize the data. Some visuals may be more appropriate than others, and in some cases, no visual may be the best alternative.

EXAMPLE 1:   *Brassica* seeds were placed on filter paper saturated with pH 1, 2, 3, or 4 buffered solutions. The positive control was filter paper saturated with water. After 2 days, 100% of the seeds in the positive control germinated. No seeds germinated in any of the buffered solutions.

POSSIBLE
SOLUTION: **No visual** is needed because the results can be summarized in one sentence: "After 2 days, 100% of the seeds that imbibed water germinated, but none of the seeds that were treated with buffered solutions pH 1, 2, 3, or 4 germinated."

EXAMPLE 2:   Light-sensitive lettuce seeds placed on filter paper saturated with water were exposed to the same fluence of white fluorescent, red, far-red, green, and blue light treatments as well as darkness, and the percentage that germinated was determined 30 hours later.

POSSIBLE
SOLUTION: Since some of the data are qualitative rather than quantitative (colors rather than wave-lengths of light), either a *table* or a *bar graph* (Figure 4.10) works well to display the results.

(A)   Table 1 Effect of light treatment on percentage of light-sensitive lettuce seeds germinated after 30 hr

Light treatment	Seed germination (%)
Red	76
White	65
Blue	44
Far-red	38
Green	37
Dark	30

(B)

Figure 1 Effect of light treatment on percentage of light-sensitive lettuce

Figure 4.10 Example 2 data summarized in (A) a table or (B) a bar graph. The positive and negative controls are placed to the left, and, if there is no particular order to the categories (colors in this example), arrange the bars in order of the longest to the shortest (or vice versa).

INAPPROPRIATE: A *line graph* is **not** appropriate because the exact wavelengths of light to which the seeds were exposed are not known. *Text only* is **not** appropriate because listing the seed germination percentages in a sentence is tedious to read and hard to comprehend.

EXAMPLE 3:   Blackworms were exposed to different concentrations of a caffeine solution for 15 minutes. The pulsation rate of the dorsal blood vessel was measured before and after treatment and the raw data were expressed as percent change in pulsation rate (negative if the rate decreased and positive if it increased).

POSSIBLE
SOLUTION: Whenever *different concentrations* of the same drug, hormone, or solution are tested, think **dose-response curve**. A dose-response curve is a *line graph* that depicts the dose (independent variable) on the *x*-axis and the response (dependent variable) on the *y*-axis (Figure 4.11). The data points were purposely not connected to show variability in pulsation rate at the same concentration of caffeine (due to variability among blackworms or variability among student measurement of pulsation rate).

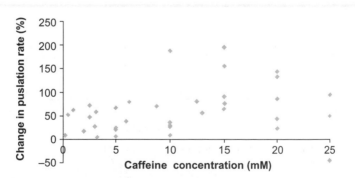

Figure 1 Effect of caffeine on pulsation rate of blackworms.

Figure 4.11 When the datadata points are not connected, the line graph is called a scatter plot.

EXAMPLE 4: The activity of an enzyme (catalase) was monitored at nine different temperatures in order to determine the optimal temperature for maximum activity.

POSSIBLE SOLUTION: If your emphasis is on the actual numbers rather than the trend, then display the results in a *table*. If the trend is more important than the numbers, use a *line graph and connect the points* with smoothed or straight lines (Figure 4.12).

(A)

Table 1 Effect of temperature on catalase activity

Temperature (°C)	Catalase activity (units of product formed · sec^{-1})
4	0.039
15	0.073
23	0.077
30	0.096
37	0.082
50	0.04
60	0.007
70	0
100	0

(B)

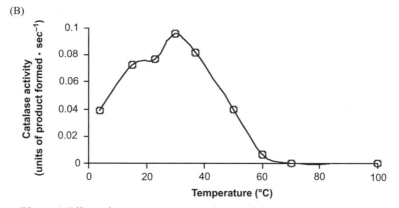

Figure 1 Effect of temperature on catalase activity

Figure 4.12 Example 4 data summarized in (A) a table or (B) a line graph. When data are summarized in a table, the emphasis is placed on the numbers rather than on the trend. For the same data, a line graph is more effective than a table in showing the trend.

Standard curves. Standard curves represent a *special case of line graph* in which the goal of the analysis is to predict one variable when the other is known. At first the data points are plotted as a scatter plot, and then a linear regression line (trendline) is fitted to the points. The degree to which the trendline actually fits the data is given by the R-squared value, whereby the closer the R-squared value is to 1, the better the correlation or fit.

To make a standard curve for a protein assay, such as the Biuret assay or the Bradford assay, a scientist prepares known concentrations of a standard protein solution (such as bovine serum albumin) and then measures the absorbance of each solution using a spectrophotometer. The relationship between absorbance and concentration is expected to be linear (Figure 4.13), as expressed in Beer's law.

To predict the protein concentration in an "unknown" solution, the scientist measures the absorbance of the solution, and then predicts the protein concentration using the regression equation of the standard curve.

Figure 4.13 Bradford standard curve constructed with absorbance data for known concentrations of BSA. The R^2 value indicates that the linear regression line fits the data very well. The absorbance of a solution with unknown protein concentration is then measured, and the absorbance is substituted into the regression equation for y to determine x (protein concentration).

Think Ahead to the Discussion

As you describe the important findings of your investigation, think about what you already know about the subject. Are the results expected? Do they agree with the findings of other investigators?

- If **yes**, then you can jot down your ideas to use in the Discussion section.
- If no, try to develop possible explanations for the results. Some reasons to consider are:
  - Human error (failure to follow the procedure, failure to use the equipment properly, failure to prepare solutions correctly, variability when multiple lab partners measure the same thing, and simple arithmetic errors). If you suspect that human error may have influenced your results, it is important to explain its contribution.
  - Numerical values were entered incorrectly in the computer plotting program.
  - Sample size was too small.
  - Variability was too great to draw any conclusions.

If you can rule out these possibilities, discuss your results with your lab partner, teaching assistant, or instructor. If there is an obvious error, an "outsider" may be able to spot it immediately. Furthermore, informal discussions may help you clarify what you know and what you do not know about the topic.

Equations

Equations are neither tables nor figures. They should be set off from the rest of the text on a separate line. If you have several equations and need to refer to them unambiguously in the body of the Results (or other) section, number each equation sequentially and place the number in parentheses on the right margin. For example:

$$\text{Absorbance} = -\log T \qquad (1)$$

If you are presenting a sequence of calculations, align the = symbol in each line, as in the following example.

Protein concentration of the unknown sample was determined using the equation of the Biuret standard curve. The measured absorbance value was substituted for y, and the equation was solved for x (the protein concentration):

$$y = 0.0417x$$
$$0.225 = 0.0417x$$
$$5.40 = x$$

Thus, the protein concentration of the sample was 5.40 mg/mL.

Make Connections

Now that the "meat" of your report is done, it's time to describe how your work fits into the existing body of knowledge. These connections are made in the Discussion and Introduction sections.

Write the Discussion

The Discussion section gives you the opportunity to **interpret your results and explain why they are important**. For a strong Discussion section:

- Summarize the results in a way that provides evidence for your conclusions. Do not use the word "prove" when discussing your results:

    FAULTY: These results prove that my hypothesis is correct.

    REVISION: These results provide support for my hypothesis.

- State how your results relate to existing knowledge (cite literature sources).
- Point out any inconsistencies in your data. This is preferable to concealing an anomalous result.
- Discuss possible sources of error.
- Describe future extensions of the current work.

Write the Introduction

The Introduction concisely states what motivated the study, how it fits into the existing body of knowledge, and the objectives of the work. The introduction consists of two primary parts: (1) background information from the literature that relates directly to the work and (2) objectives of the current work.

After having written drafts of the Materials and Methods, Results, and Discussion sections, you should be intimately familiar with the procedure, the data, and what the data mean. Now you are in a position to put your investigation into perspective. What was already known about the topic? Were there any inconsistencies or unanswered questions? Why did you carry out this investigation?

If you designed your own experiment based on the scientific method, you probably answered these questions already. If this investigation was a laboratory exercise prepared by your instructor, reread the exercise to see if some of these questions have already been answered. The idea is not to copy the laboratory exercise introduction verbatim, but to make sure you understand the objectives.

Use keywords from the objectives to locate background information in the literature (see Chapter 2). Evaluate the titles in the search results critically to make sure the sources are relevant to your investigation.

The opening sentence of the Introduction section is usually a general observation or result familiar to the audience. By convention, generally accepted statements are written in present tense (see "Present Tense or Past Tense?" in Chapter 5). Subsequent sentences narrow down the topic to the specific focus of the current investigation. Subsequent paragraphs then provide background information from the literature and describe unanswered questions or inconsistencies. The objectives of the current work are usually stated in past tense in the last paragraph of the Introduction section.

Effective Advertising

The whole point of writing your paper is to communicate your work to your peers. The Abstract and the Title are the primary tools your audience will use to decide whether or not they are interested in your work.

Write the Abstract

The abstract is a **summary of the entire paper** in 250 words or less. It contains:

- An introduction (scope and purpose)
- A short description of the methods
- The results
- Your conclusions

There are no literature citations or references to figures in the Abstract.

After the title, the Abstract is the most important part of the scientific paper used by the reader to determine initial interest in the author's work. Abstracts are indexed in databases that catalogue the literature in the biological sciences. If an abstract suggests that the author's work may be relevant to your own work, you will probably want to read the whole article. On the other hand, if an abstract is vague or essential information is missing, you will probably decide that the paper is not worth reading. When you write the Abstract for your own laboratory report, put yourself in the position of the reader. If you want the reader to be interested in your work, write an effective Abstract.

Writing the Abstract is difficult because you have to condense your entire paper into 250 words or less. One strategy for doing this is to list the key points of each section, as though you were taking notes on your own paper. Then write the key points in full sentences. Revise the draft for clarity and conciseness using strategies such as using active voice, combining choppy sentences with connecting words, rewording run-on sentences, and eliminating redundancy. With each revision, look for ways to shorten the text so that the resulting Abstract is a concise and accurate summary of your work.

The ability to write abstracts is important to a scientist's career. Should you someday wish to present your research at an academic society meeting, such as the Society for Neuroscience, the American Association for the Advancement of Science, or the National Association of Biology Teachers (to name just a few), you will be asked to submit an abstract of your presentation to the committee in charge of the meeting program. Your chances of being among the select field of presenters at these meetings are much better if you have learned to write a clear and intelligent abstract.

Write the Title

The Title is a **short, informative description** of the essence of the paper. You may choose a working title when you begin to write your paper, but revise the title after subsequent drafts. Remember that readers use the title to determine initial interest in the paper, so descriptive accuracy is the most essential element of your title. Brevity is nice if it can be achieved. Some journals (especially the British ones) are fond of puns and humor in their titles, but this kind of thing may be better left for later in your career.

Here are some examples of vague and nondescriptive titles:

> **FAULTY:** Quantitative Protein Analysis

> **FAULTY:** The Assessment of Protein Content in an Unknown Sample

> **FAULTY:** Egg White Protein Analysis

These titles leave the reader wondering what method of protein analysis was used and what sample was analyzed.

> **REVISION:** Assessment of Protein Concentration in Egg White Using the Biuret Method

Documenting Sources

References are typically cited in the Introduction and Discussion sections of a scientific paper, and the procedures given in Materials and Methods are often modifications of those in previous work. Citation and reference format in the sciences differs from that in the humanities in two important ways:

- It is not customary to use direct quotations in scientific papers; paraphrase instead.
- In the citation in the text, it is not customary to give the page number(s) of the source; instead, use one of the two citation systems explained in the following section.

The References section is also called *Works Cited* or *Literature Cited*, because it includes only the published sources you cited in your paper. It is not a "bibliography" or a list of works consulted to learn more about the topic.

Citation and Reference Formats

Whenever you use another person's ideas, whether they are published or not, you must document the source. This is done by citing the source in an abbreviated form in the text and then giving the full reference in the References section at the end of the document (only sources that have been cited in the text may be included in the References section). An exception to this practice is personal communications, usually from an expert in the field that shares unpublished observations. These are cited in the text, but are not listed under References.

The CSE Manual (2006) recommends using the Citation-Sequence System (C-S) or the Name-Year System (N-Y) for documenting your sources. The system you actually use depends on your instructor's preference or on the format specified by the particular scientific journal in which you aspire to publish.

Examples of the same passage of text documented using the C-S and N-Y formats are given in Table 4.3. Notice in both examples how inconspicuously the source is documented. This style is quite different from that practiced in some disciplines in the humanities, in which the source may be introduced at length in the text—for example: "According to Warne and Hickock in their 1989 paper published in *Plant Physiology*, antheridiogen may be related to the gibberellins." **Do not use this style in your lab reports!**

With regard to the full reference, the two formats differ in the sequence of information and the listing of the month of publication. In the N-Y system, the year of publication follows the author's name; in the C-S system, the year follows the journal name. The month of publication is only used in C-S format.

The Name-Year system has the advantage that people working in the field will know the literature and, on seeing the authors' names, will understand the reference without having to check the reference list. With the citation-sequence system, the reader must turn to the reference list at the end of the paper to gain the same information. The important thing, however, is to choose a citation format and adhere to it consistently throughout your paper.

The Citation-Sequence System

In the Citation-Sequence (C-S) system (Table 4.4, p. 61), the source is cited with a number in parentheses following the paraphrased sentence (in some journals, this number is in square brackets or displayed as a super-scripted endnote, but never a footnote). On the page of references at the end of the document, the citations are listed in **numerical order** and include the full reference.

The Name-Year System

In the Name-Year (N-Y) system (Table 4.4, p. 62), the source is given in the form of author(s) and year. The source may be cited in parentheses or as the subject of the sentence, as shown in the following examples:

PARENTHESES: C-fern gametophytes respond to antheridio-gen only for a short time after inoculation (Banks et al. 1993).

AS THE SUBJECT: Banks et al. (1993) found that C-fern gametophytes respond to antheridiogen only for a short time after inoculation.

The **number of authors** determines how the authors are cited in N-Y system (Table 4.4).

On the page of references at the end of the document, the references are listed in **alphabetical order** according to the first author's last name. The last name is written first, followed by the initials. When there are 10 or fewer authors, list all authors' names. When there are more than 10 authors, list the first 10 and then write *et al.* after the tenth name.

The reference styles for the Citation-Sequence and Name-Year formats are summarized in the boxes on pages 61 and 62.

Reference Formats

TABLE 4.3 Two systems of source documentation used in scientific papers

C-S REFERENCE FORMAT

The references are listed **in the order they are cited**. The author's last name is written first, followed by the initials. When there are 10 or fewer authors, list all authors' names. When there are more than 10 authors, list the first 10 and then write *et al.* after the tenth name.

Journal article	Number of the citation. First author's last name First initials, Subsequent authors' names separated by commas. Article title. Journal title Year Month; Volume number(issue number): inclusive pages.
Article in book	Number of the citation. First author's last name First initials, Subsequent authors' names separated by commas. Article title. In: Editors' names followed by a comma and the word *editors*. Book title, edition. Place of Publication: Publisher; Year of publication. pp inclusive pages.
Book	Number of the citation. First author's or editor's last name First initials, Subsequent authors' or editors' names separated by commas. Title of book. Place of Publication: Publisher; Year of publication. Total number of pages in book followed by *p*.

Note: If you cite more than one paper published by the same author in *different* years, list them in chronological order: (Dawson 2001, 2003). If you cite more than one paper published by the same author in the *same* year, add a letter after the year: "…was described in recent work by Dawson (1999a, 1999b)."

Electronic Journal Articles

The citation in the text is the same as for printed sources:

        C-S   …confirmed in a previous study (1).

        N-Y   …was confirmed in a previous study by Banks (1994).

Reference Formats

TABLE 4.3 *Continued*

N-Y REFERENCE FORMAT
The references are listed in **alphabetical order**. The last name is written first, followed by the initials. When there are 10 or fewer authors, list all authors' names. When there are more than 10 authors, list the first 10 and then write *et al.* after the tenth name. Type references with hanging indent format.

Journal article	First author's last name First initials, Subsequent authors' names separated by commas. Year of publication. Article title. Journal title Volume number(issue number): inclusive pages.
Article in book	First author's last name First initials, Subsequent authors' names separated by commas. Year of publication. Article title. In: Editors' names followed by a comma and the word *editors*. Book title, edition. Place of Publication: Publisher. pp inclusive pages.
Book	First author's or editor's last name First initials, Subsequent authors' or editors' names separated by commas. Year of publication. Title of book. Place of Publication: Publisher. Total number of pages in book followed by *p*.

Reference Formats

The full reference at the end of the document begins with the same information that would be provided for a printed source. However, if the source is exclusively online, then the URL and date accessed is placed at the end of the reference. It is absolutely essential to include the date accessed, because documents on the Web may move or be removed altogether. For example, the USDA PLANTS Database is entirely online. If you included information about a plant from the database on September 13, 2008, then you would reference it as follows:

> **C-S** 1. USDA, NRCS. The PLANTS Database. 2008. <http://plants.usda.gov/> Accessed 2008 September 13.

> **N-Y**   USDA, NRCS. 2008. The PLANTS Database.
> <http://plants.usda.gov> Accessed 2008
> September 13.

Sources from the Internet and the World Wide Web

Ease of access to the latest information makes the World Wide Web an irresistible source for nearly everything. Scientific communications are no exception. Take heed, however; information retrieved from the Internet and the World Wide Web may be unreliable. The authors of the communication, not journal editors or copy editors, are responsible for the accuracy of the contents. Because there is no review from an outside source, mistakes can occur. For this reason, it is preferable to cite only reliably published books or peer-reviewed articles in your laboratory report.

In some instances, sources from the Web may be used to support published findings. Use one of the two citation formats described previously. If the author is not known, find an alternate source. If there is no date of publication, cite the date of modification; if neither of these dates is given, use the date accessed. For example:

> **C-S**   …is recommended by the Counselling Services
> at the University of Victoria (1).

> **N-Y**   …is recommended by the Counselling Services
> at the University of Victoria (*How to Read*
> *University Texts*, 2001).

The full reference at the end of the document would follow the format given in "Electronic Journal Articles," with the same information that would be provided for a printed source plus the URL and the date accessed.

For more information on using Internet sources, see Harnack and Kleppinger (2001).

TABLE 4.4 Examples of source documentation used in scientific papers

CITATION-SEQUENCE SYSTEM	
	TEXT CITATIONS
Sources are listed in the order they are cited	Gametophytes of the tropical fern *Ceratopteris richardii* (C-fern) develop either as males or hermaphrodites. Their fate is determined by the pheromone antheridiogen (1, 2). Gametophytes respond to antheridiogen only for a short time between 3 and 4 days after inoculation (3). Although the structure of antheridiogen is unknown, it is thought to be related to the gibberellins (4). Gibberellins are a group of plant hormones involved in stem elongation, seed germination, flowering, and fruit development (5).
	CORRESPONDING FULL REFERENCES
Article in book	1. Näf U. Antheridiogens and antheridial development. In: Dyer AF, editor. The Experimental Biology of Ferns. London: Academic Press; 1979. pp. 436-470.
Journal article	2. Näf U, Nakanishi K, Endo M. On the physiology and chemistry of fern antheridiogens. Bot. Rev. 1975 Jul-Sep; 41(3): 315-359.
Journal article	3. Banks J, Webb M, Hickok L. Programming of sexual phenotype in the homosporous fern *Ceratopteris richardii*. Inter. J. Plant Sci. 1993 Dec; 154(4): 522-534.
Journal article	4. Warne T, Hickok L. Evidence for a gibberellin biosynthetic origin of *Ceratopteris* antheridiogen. Plant Physiol. 1989 Feb; 89(2): 535-538.
Book	5. Treshow M. Environment and Plant Response. New York: McGraw-Hill; 1970. 250 p.

Book references give the total number of pages in the book, not the pages from which you extracted the information

Reference Formats

TABLE 4.4 *Continued*

NAME-YEAR SYSTEM	
	TEXT CITATIONS
1 author 3 or more authors 2 authors 1 author	Gametophytes of the tropical fern *Ceratopteris richardii* (C-fern) develop either as males or hermaphrodites. Their fate is determined by the pheromone antheridiogen (Näf 1979; Näf et al. 1975). Banks et al. (1993) found that gametophytes respond to antheridiogen only for a short time between 3 and 4 days after inoculation. Although the structure of antheridiogen is unknown, it is thought to be related to the gibberellins (Warne and Hickok 1989). Gibberellins are a group of plant hormones involved in stem elongation, seed germination, flowering, and fruit development (Treshow 1970).
	CORRESPONDING FULL REFERENCES
Journal article	Banks J, Webb M, and Hickok L. 1993. Programming of sexual phenotype in the homosporous fern *Cera-topteris richardii*. Inter. J. Plant Sci. 154(4): 522-534.
Article in book	Näf U. 1979. Antheridiogens and antheridial development. In: Dyer AF, editor. The Experimental Biology of Ferns. London: Academic Press. pp. 436-470.
Journal article	Näf U, Nakanishi K, and Endo M. 1975. On the physiology and chemistry of fern antheridiogens. Bot. Rev. 41(3): 315-359.
Book	Treshow M. 1970. Environment and Plant Response. New York: McGraw-Hill. 250 p.
Journal article	Warne T and Hickok L. 1989. Evidence for a gibberellin biosynthetic origin of *Ceratopteris* antheridiogen. Plant Physiol. 89(2): 535-538.

Chapter 5

REVISION

Revision—reading your paper and making corrections and improvements—is an important task that usually does not get nearly the attention it deserves. Too many students write the first draft of their laboratory report the night before it is due and hand in the hard copy, still warm from the printer, without even having proofread it.

The truth is, most writers cannot produce a clear, concise, and error-free product on the first try. It may take several revisions before the writer is satisfied that he or she has conveyed, with clarity and logic, the motivation for writing the paper, the important findings, and the conclusions. For this reason, **prepare the first draft as early as possible** so that you will have the time to think about it, get help if necessary, get feedback from your peer reviewer, and make final revisions.

Getting Ready to Revise

Take a Break

The first step in revision is *not* to do it immediately after you have written the first draft. You need to distance yourself from the paper to gain the objectivity needed to read the paper critically. So take a break, and get a good night's sleep.

Look at the Big Picture

In the early stages of the revision process, content is more important than format. Make sure you have answered all the questions in the laboratory exercise (if applicable), and use the "Biology Lab Report Checklist" (pp. 92–93) and/or the assignment rubric (course website) to make sure each section of your laboratory report contains the proper content. Don't worry about whether or not a table caption is in the right position until you are sure you even need to include the table.

Ask yourself the following questions:

- What are the goals and objectives of this paper? Did I make these objectives clear to the reader?
- What questions and concerns do I have with this draft? What are some ways I can begin to address these concerns?
- What parts need feedback (not sure if my meaning is clear, not sure if I understood this concept correctly, and other issues)?
- What do I like about this paper? What are its strengths and what has gone well?

Be prepared to discuss your answers to these questions with your peer reviewer. Peer review is the next step in the revision process.

Get Feedback

When we are engrossed in our work, we may fail to recognize that what is obvious to us is not obvious to an "outsider." Some typical problem areas are flow and organization of the paper and typographical or grammatical errors.

That is where feedback from someone who is familiar with the subject matter comes in handy. Ask a peer to review your paper. Return the favor by reviewing his or hers.

Tips for being a good peer reviewer. There are two issues with which you may struggle when you are asked to review someone's paper: (1) I'm not confident that I know the "right" answer or know enough about the writing process to give good suggestions, and (2) I don't want to hurt the writer's feelings. These are valid concerns, and resolving them will require, first, a willingness to learn as much about writing scientific papers as possible, and second, the attitude that if something is unclear to you, it may also be unclear to other readers. With each paper you review, you will gain more confidence in your ability to give constructive feedback. In the meantime, however, a good rule of thumb is to give the kinds of suggestions and consideration that you would like to receive on your own paper.

There are two schools of thought concerning how the reviewer should provide feedback on the paper. One is that no marks should be made on the paper itself; instead, any comments should be written on a separate sheet of paper. The second school of thought is just the opposite. Although the first method respects the writer's ownership of the paper, it is not very practical. First of all, it is difficult to describe exactly where on the paper the revision should be made. Secondly, vague suggestions like "improve flow of introduction" are not nearly as helpful to a peer as "what do you mean by…" and then circle or underline the confusing phrase. Think of the peer review process as a team sport: you are not challenging your teammate's right to be on the team. You are working together to get the best possible result.

Here are some concrete tips for being a good peer reviewer:

- Talk to the writer about his or her objectives, questions and concerns, parts that need specific feedback, and perceived strengths and weaknesses.

- Use the "Biology Lab Report Checklist" for content.

- Use a pencil and standard proofreader's marks to mark awkward sentences, spelling and punctuation mistakes, and formatting errors. Do not feel you have to rewrite individual sentences—that is the writer's job.

- Ask questions. Let the writer know where you can't follow his/her thinking, where you need more examples, where you expect more detailed analysis, and so on.

- Do not be embarrassed about making lots of comments; the author does not have to accept your suggestions. On the other hand, if you say only good things about the paper, how will the writer know whether the paper is accomplishing the desired objectives?

You can fine-tune your proofreading skills on any text. You may recognize some of your own problems in other people's writing, and with persistence and practice, you will find creative solutions to correct these problems. Keep a log of the problems that recur in your writing and review them from time to time. Repetition builds awareness, which will help you achieve greater clarity in your writing.

Have an informal discussion with your peer reviewer. Sometimes the comments made by the peer reviewer on the paper are self-explanatory. Other times, however, the peer reviewer cannot respond to certain parts of the paper, because more information is required. Under these circumstances, an informal discussion between the writer and the reviewer is helpful. There are two important rules for this discussion:

- First, the writer talks and the reviewer listens. The objective is to help the writer express exactly what he/she wants to say in the paper.

- Second, the reviewer talks, in nonjudgmental terms, about which parts of the paper were readily understandable and which parts were confusing. The reviewer does not have to be an experienced writer to do this—no two people have exactly the same life experiences, and there is always something positive you can learn from looking at your writing from someone else's perspective.

Revise Again

The comments provided by your peer reviewer, both on your paper and during the subsequent informal discussion, should give you some ideas on how your paper can be improved. The areas that require attention will most likely fall into one of the following categories:

1. Conventions in biology
2. Numbers
3. Standard abbreviations
4. Punctuation
5. Clarity
6. Grammar
7. Word usage
8. Spelling
9. Global revision

1. Conventions in Biology

Audience. Scientific papers are written by scientists for fellow scientists. When you write your laboratory reports, write for your fellow students as though they are scientists, not students in a classroom setting. Even though your instructor will be the one who reads and evaluates your reports, think of him or her as a mentor, not the audience.

> EXAMPLE: The purpose of this experiment ~~is to teach the student how~~ <u>was</u> to determine the protein concentration in an unknown sample.

The audience has a knowledge base similar to the author of the paper. Thus, when you introduce your topic and describe and interpret your results, you should assume that your audience will know some scientific vocabulary, but that you should clarify or define less-familiar terms. When deciding on how much background information to include, assume that your audience knows what you learned in class.

Do not use jargon (terms known only to experts) or copy sections of journal articles because you think that your own words are inferior to those of experts in the field. The objective of your writing is not to impress your instructor with empty words, but to enable your peers to understand what you have accomplished.

Introductions. In some fields, the author attempts to attract a large audience for his or her paper by asking an intriguing question or presenting a dilemma to capture the reader's interest. In scientific papers, however, the author assumes that the audience is already interested in the subject. Readers of scientific papers typically determine initial interest in a paper from the title and the abstract. If these sections seem promising, the reader will then peruse the Introduction to determine further interest. There is no need for the author to pique the reader's interest with longwinded introductions, because the interest is already there.

When you write the Introduction section of your laboratory report, just jump right in with your topic. Eliminate unnecessary introductions such as the first sentence in the following example:

EXAMPLE: ~~In many areas of biology, it is important to gain a higher understanding of enzyme activity.~~ Rate of enzyme activity depends on factors such as enzyme concentration, substrate concentration, pH, temperature, and the presence of inhibitors.

Get to the point. Describe what area of enzyme activity you studied, why, and what you expected to learn from your work.

You may be tempted to go overboard with detail in the Results section of your report, as illustrated by the following example:

EXAMPLE: ~~From the data that has been gathered, a graph depicting the effect of various pH environments on the rate of catalase activity is represented. The graph displays the pH tested and the reaction rate. The data plotted is an accumulation of data from several lab sections. Through analyzing the graph I can see that~~ <u>T</u>there ~~is~~ <u>was</u> no activity below a pH of 4 or above 10. Maximum catalase activity occurred at pH 7.

Cut to the chase—don't waste the reader's time with sentences that say nothing substantive.

Initially it is difficult to write in (and read) the terse, get-to-the-point style that characterizes scientific papers. With practice, however, you may come to appreciate this style, because in a well-written paper, not a word is wasted. The benefit to you as a reader is that you extract a maximum amount of information from a minimum amount of text.

Present tense or past tense? In scientific papers, present tense is used mainly in the following situations:

- To make generally accepted statements (for example, "Photo-syn-thesis *is* the process whereby green plants produce sugars.")
- When referring directly to a table or figure in your paper (for example, "Figure 1 *is* a schematic diagram of the apparatus.")
- When you state the findings of published authors (for example, "Catalase HPII from *E. coli is* highly resistant to denaturation (Switala and others, 1999).")

Past tense is used mainly in the following situations:

- To report your own work, especially in the Abstract, Materials and Methods, and Results sections, because it remains to be seen if it is accepted as fact (for example, "At temperatures above 37°C, catalase activity *decreased.*").
- To cite another author's findings directly (for example, "Miller and others (1998) *found* that…").

Active and passive voice. In **active voice**, the subject *performs* the action. In **passive voice**, the subject *receives* the action. Consider the following example:

PASSIVE: The clam was opened by the sea star.
[Emphasis on *clam*]

ACTIVE: The sea star opened the clam.
[Emphasis on *sea star*]

Although the meaning is the same in both sentences, notice the difference in emphasis. In active voice, the emphasis is on the performer, and the action takes place in the direction the reader reads the sentence. Active voice is recommended by most style guides for reasons that include the following:

- It sounds more natural and is easier for the reader to process.
- It is shorter and more dynamic.

- There is no ambiguity about who/what the subject of the sentence is, or about who did the action.

Consider the following example:

PASSIVE: It was concluded from this observation that...

ACTIVE: I concluded from this observation that...

Passive voice leaves the reader wondering who drew the conclusion; active voice conveys this information clearly.

While active voice is generally preferred, passive voice may be more appropriate when *what* is being done is more important than *who* is doing it. For example:

PASSIVE: Catalase was extracted from a potato.
[Emphasis on *catalase*]

ACTIVE: I extracted catalase from a potato.
[Emphasis on *I*]

Notice the difference in emphasis. Is it really important to the success of the procedure that *you* did it, or does the emphasis belong on the catalase?

A paper that contains a mixture of active and passive voice is pleasant to read. Your decision to use active or passive voice in a sentence should ultimately be determined by clarity and brevity. In other words, use active voice to emphasize the subject and the fact that the subject is performing the action. Use passive voice when the action is more important than who is doing it.

2. Numbers

Numbers are used for quantitative measurements. In the past, numbers less than 10 were spelled out, and larger numbers were written as numerals. The modern scientific number style recommended in the upcoming Seventh Edition of the CBE Manual (<http://www.councilscienceeditors.org/publications/ssf_numberstyle.cfm>, accessed 2004 Jan 31) aims for a more consistent usage of numbers. The new rules are as follows:

a. Use numerals to express any *quantity*. This form increases their visibility in scientific writing, and emphasizes their importance.
   - Cardinal numbers, for example, 3 observations, 5 samples, 2 times

- In conjunction with a unit, for example, 5 g, 0.5 mm, 37°C, 50%, 1 hr. Pay attention to spacing, capitalization, and punctuation (see Table 5.1).
- Mathematical relationships, for example, 1:5 dilution, 1000× magnification, 10-fold

b. Spell out numbers in the following cases:

- When the number begins a sentence, for example, *"Fifty g of potatoes was [not were] homogenized."* rather than *"50 g of potatoes was homogenized."* Alternatively, restructure the sentence so that the number does not begin the sentence. Notice that when numbers are used in conjunction with units, the quantity is considered to be singular, not plural.
- When there are two adjacent numbers, retain the numeral that goes with the unit, and spell out the other one. An example of this is *The solution was divided into four 250-mL flasks.*
- When the number is used in a nonquantitative sense, for example, *one of the treatments, the expression approaches zero, one is required to consider…*
- When the number is an ordinal number less than 10, and when the number expresses rank rather than quantity, for example, *the second time, was first discovered.*

c. Use scientific notation for very large or very small numbers. For the number 5,000,000, write 5×10^6, not *5 million.* For the number *0.000005*, write 5×10^{-6}. Remember to always report values with the correct significant figures. This should reflect the precision with which the number was derived.

d. For decimal numbers less than one, always mark the ones column with a zero. For example, write *0.05*, not *.05.*

3. Standard Abbreviations

The CBE Manual (1994) defines standard abbreviations for authors and publishers in the sciences and mathematics. Some of the terms and abbreviations that you may encounter in introductory biology courses are shown in Table 5.1. Take note of spacing, case (capital or lowercase letters), and punctuation use. Except where noted, the symbols are the same for singular and plural terms (for example, 30 min *not* 30 mins).

4. Punctuation

The purpose of punctuation marks is to divide sentences and parts of sentences to make the meaning clear. A few of the most common punctuation marks and their uses are described in the following section. For a more comprehensive, but still concise, treatment of punctuation, see Hacker (1997), Lunsford (2001), or Lunsford and Connors (1995, 1999).

The comma. The comma inserts a pause in the sentence in order to avoid confusion. Note the ambiguity in the following sentence:

> While the sample was incubating the students prepared the solutions for the experiment.

A comma *should* be used in the following situations:

a. To connect two independent clauses that are joined by *and, but, or, nor, for, so,* or *yet.* An independent clause contains a subject and a verb, and can stand alone as a sentence.

   EXAMPLE: Feel free to call me at home, but don't call after 9 P.M.

b. After an introductory clause, to separate the clause from the main body of the sentence.

   EXAMPLE: Although she spent many hours writing her lab report, she earned a low grade because she forgot to answer the questions in the laboratory exercise.

   A comma is not needed if the clause is short.

   EXAMPLE: Suddenly, the power went out.

c. Between items in a series, including the last two.

   EXAMPLE: Enzyme activity is affected by factors such as substrate concentration, pH, temperature, and salt.

d. Between coordinate adjectives (if the adjectives can be connected with *and*)

   EXAMPLE: The students' original, humorous remarks made my class today particularly enjoyable. [*Original and humorous remarks* makes sense.]

   A comma is not needed if the adjectives are cumulative (if the adjectives cannot be connected with *and*).

   EXAMPLE: The three, tall, muscular students look like football players. [It would sound strange to say *three and tall and muscular students.*]

TABLE 5.1 Standard abbreviations in scientific writing

TERM	SYMBOL OR ABBREVIATION	EXAMPLE
Latin words and phrases		
circa (approximately)	ca.	The lake is ca. 300 m deep.
et alii (and others)	*et al.*	Jones *et al.* (1999) found that …
et cetera (and so forth)	etc.	pH, alkalinity, etc. were measured.
exempli gratia (for example)	e.g.	Water quality characteristics (e.g., pH, alkalinity) were measured.
id est (that is)	i.e.	The enzyme was denatured at high temperatures, i.e., the enzyme activity was zero.
nota bene (take notice)	NB	NB: Never add water to acid when making a solution.
Length		
nanometer (10^{-9} meter)	nm	450 nm, 10 µm, 2.5 cm
micron (10^{-6} meter)	µm	
millimeter (10^{-3} meter)	mm	*Note:* There is a space between the number and the abbreviation. There is no period after the abbreviation.
centimeter (10^{-2} meter)	cm	
meter	m	
Mass		
nanogram (10^{-9} gram)	ng	450 ng, 100 µg, 2.5 g, 10 kg
microgram (10^{-6} gram)	µg	
milligram (10^{-3} gram)	mg	*Note:* There is a space between the number and the abbreviation. There is no period after the abbreviation.
gram	g	
kilogram (10^{3} gram)	kg	

TABLE 5.1 *Continued*

TERM	SYMBOL OR ABBREVIATION	EXAMPLE
Volume		
microliter (10^{-6} liter)	µl or µL	450 µl or 450 µL, 0.45 ml or 0.45 mL, 2 l or 2 L
milliliter (10^{-3} liter)	ml or mL	
liter	l or L	*Note:* There is a space between the number and the abbreviation. There is no period after the abbreviation.
cubic centimeter (ca. 1 mL)	cm³	
Time		
seconds	s or sec	60 s or 60 sec, 60 min, 24 h or 24 hr, 1 d
minutes	min	
hours	h or hr	*Note:* There is a space between the number and the abbreviation. There is no period after the abbreviation (unless the unit ends a sentence).
days	d	
Concentration		TBS contains 0.01 M Tris-HCl, pH 7.4 and 0.15 M NaCl.
molar (U.S. use)	M	
molar (SI units)	mol L^{-1}	Brine shrimp can be raised in 35 ppt seawater.
parts per thousand	ppt	
Other		
degree(s) Celsius	°C	15° C
degree(s) Fahrenheit	°F	59° F
figure, figures	Fig., Figs.	As shown by Fig. 1, …
foot-candle	fc or ft-c	500 fc or 500 ft-c
mole	mol	
percent	%	95% (no space between number and symbol)
species (sing.)	sp.	*Tetrahymena* sp.
species (plur.)	spp.	*Tetrahymena* spp.

e. With *which*, but not *that* (see Word usage: that, which)

f. To set off conjunctive adverbs such as *however, therefore, more-over, consequently, instead, likewise, nevertheless, similarly, subse-quently, accordingly,* and *finally*

> **EXAMPLE:**   Instructors expect students to hand in their work on time; however, illness and personal emergencies are acceptable excuses.

g. To set off transitional expressions such as *for example, as a result, in conclusion, in other words, on the contrary,* and *on the other hand*

> **EXAMPLE:**   Chuck participates in many extracurricular activities in college. As a result, he rarely gets enough sleep.

h. To set off parenthetical expressions. Parenthetical expressions are statements that provide additional information; however, they interrupt the flow of the sentence.

> **EXAMPLE:**   Fluency in a foreign language, as we all know, requires years of instruction and practice.

A comma *should not* be used in the following situations.

- After *that*, when *that* is used in an introductory clause

> **EXAMPLE:**   The student could not believe that he lost points on his laboratory report because of a few spelling mistakes.

- Between cumulative adjectives, which are adjectives that would not make sense if separated by the word *and* (see Item 4 in preceding list)

The semicolon. The semicolon inserts a stop between two independent clauses not joined by a coordinating conjunction (*and, but, or, nor, for, so,* or *yet*). Each independent clause (one that contains a subject and a verb) could stand alone as a sentence, but the semicolon indicates a closer relationship between the clauses than if they were written as separate sentences.

> **EXAMPLE:**   Outstanding student-athletes use their time wisely; this trait makes them highly sought after by employers.

A semicolon is also used to separate items in a series in which the items are already separated by commas.

EXAMPLE: Participating in sports has many advantages.
First, you are doing something good for your
health; second, you enjoy the camaraderie of people with a common interest; third, you learn discipline, which helps you make effective use of
your time.

The colon. The colon is used to call attention to the words that follow it.
Some conventional uses of a colon are shown in the following examples.

Dear Sir or Madam:
5:30 P.M.
2:1 (ratio)

In references, to separate the place of publication and the publisher, as in

Sunderland, MA: Sinauer Associates, Inc.

A colon is often used to set off a list, as in the following example.

EXAMPLE: Catalase activity has been found in the following
vegetables: potatoes, leeks, parsnips, onions, zucchini, carrots, and broccoli.

A colon *should not* be used when the list follows the words *are, consist of,
such as, including,* or *for example.*

EXAMPLE: Catalase activity has been found in vegetables
such as potatoes, leeks, parsnips, onions,
zucchini, carrots, and broccoli.

The period. The period is used to end all sentences except questions and
exclamations. It is also used in some abbreviations, for example, *Mr., Ms.,
Dr., Ph.D., i.e.,* and *e.g.*

Parentheses. Parentheses are used mainly in two situations in scientific
writing: to enclose supplemental material and to enclose references to
visuals or sources. Use parentheses sparingly because they interrupt the
flow of the sentence.

EXAMPLE: Experimental error (failure to make the solutions
correctly, arithmetic errors, and failure to zero the
spectrophotometer) was the main reason for the
unexpected results.

REFERENCE
TO VISUAL: There was no catalase activity above 70°C (Figure 1).

CITATION-
SEQUENCE
SYSTEM: C-fern spores do not germinate in the dark (1).

NAME-YEAR
SYSTEM: C-fern spores do not germinate in the dark (Cooke
               and others, 1987).

The dash. The dash is used to set off material that requires special emphasis. To make a dash on the computer, type two hyphens without a space before, after or in between. In some word processing programs, the two hyphens are automatically converted to a solid dash.

Similar to commas and parentheses, a pair of dashes may be used to set off supplemental material.

EXAMPLE: Experimental error--failure to make the solutions
             correctly, arithmetic errors, and failure to zero the
             spectrophotometer--was the main reason for the
             unexpected results. (If the word processing pro-
             gram has been set up to convert the two hyphens
             to a solid dash, the sentence looks like this:
             Human error—failure to make...spectrophotome-
             ter—was the main reason...)

Similar to a colon, a single dash calls attention to the information that follows it.

EXAMPLE: Catalase activity has been found in many vegeta-
             bles–potatoes, leeks, parsnips, onions, zucchini,
             carrots, and broccoli.

If an abrupt or dramatic interruption is desired, use a dash. If the writing is more formal or the interruption should be less conspicuous, use one of the other three punctuation marks. However, do not replace a pair of dashes with commas when the material to be set off already contains commas, as in the following example.

EXAMPLE: The instruments that she plays–oboe, guitar, and
             piano–are not traditionally used in the marching band.

5. Clarity

The main reason for writing a scientific paper or laboratory report is to communicate information to your peers. If you do not present this information clearly, your readers will not understand what you mean. Lack of clarity translates into a low grade. Researchers and faculty members, whose reputation depends on the number and quality of publications, simply cannot afford *not* to write clearly, because poorly written papers may be equated with shoddy scientific methods.

There are a number of ways to improve the clarity of your writing. These include eliminating wordiness, redundancy, empty phrases, and ambiguity; reducing complexity; and ensuring good flow between sentences and paragraphs.

Eliminate wordiness. "Wordiness" means using too many words to convey an idea. One form of wordiness is **redundancy**, using two or more words that mean the same thing (Table 5.2).

Redundancy is easily corrected by eliminating one of the redundant words.

Empty phrases are another source of wordiness. Consider the following two sentences (inspired by Van Alstyne, 1986). Which one would you rather read?

EXAMPLE 1: It is absolutely essential that you use a minimum number of words in view of the fact that your reader has numerous other tasks to complete at the present time.

EXAMPLE 2: Write concisely, because your reader is busy.

Replace empty phrases with a concise alternative (Table 5.3).

TABLE 5.2 Examples of redundancy

REDUNDANT	REVISED
It is absolutely essential…	It is essential…
mutual cooperation	cooperation
basic fundamental concept	basic concept or fundamental concept
totally unique	unique
The solution was obtained and transferred…	The solution was transferred…

A third source of wordiness is **needlessly complex sentences**. Watch out for the sentence constructions illustrated by the following examples.

EXAMPLE 1: *There are* two protein assays *that* are often used in research laboratories.

REVISION: Two protein assays are often used in research laboratories. [Avoid expletives.]

EXAMPLE 2: *It is interesting to note that* some enzymes are stable at temperatures above 60°C.

REVISION: Some enzymes are stable at temperatures above 60°C. [Avoid unnecessary introductions.]

TABLE 5.3 Examples of empty phrases

EMPTY	CONCISE
a downward trend	a decrease
a great deal of	much higher
a majority of	most
accounted for the fact that	because
as a result	so, therefore
as a result of	because
as soon as	when
at which time	when
at all times	always
at a much greater rate than	faster
at the present time, at this time	now, currently
based on the fact that	because
brief in duration	short, quick
by means of	by
came to the conclusion	concluded
despite the fact that, in spite of the fact that	although, though
due to the fact that, in view of the fact that	because
for this reason	so

EXAMPLE 3: *The analyses were done on* the recombinant DNA to determine which piece of foreign DNA was inserted into the vector.

REVISION: The recombinant DNA was analyzed to determine which piece of foreign DNA was inserted into the vector. [Make *DNA,* not the *analyses,* the subject of the sentence.]

EXAMPLE 4: *We make the recommendation* that micropipettors be used to measure volumes less than 1 mL.

TABLE 5.3 *Continued*

EMPTY	CONCISE
in fact	*omit*
functions to, serves to	*omit*
degree of	higher, more
in a manner similar to	like
in the amount of	of
in the vicinity of	near, around
is dependent upon	depends on
is situated in	is in
it is interesting to note that, it is worth pointing out that	*omit these kinds of unnecessary introductions*
it is recommended	I (we) recommend
on account of	because, due to
prior to	before
provided that	if
referred to as	called
so as to	to
through the use of	by, with
with regard to	on, about
with the exception of	except
with the result that	so that

REVISION: We recommend that micropipettors be used to measure volumes less than 1 mL. [Replace sluggish noun phrases with verb phrases.]

EXAMPLE 5: These assays alone cannot tell what the protein concentration of a substance is.

REVISION: These assays alone cannot determine the protein concentration of a substance. [Replace colloquial expressions with precise alternatives.]

Eliminate ambiguity. Avoid vague use of *this, that,* and *which* when referring to topics mentioned previously. What does the writer mean by *this* and *which* in the following example?

EXAMPLE: The data show that the longer the enzyme was exposed to the salt solution, the lower the enzyme activity in the assay. *This* means that the salt changes the conformation of the enzyme, *which* makes it less reactive with the substrate.

The subsequent revision eliminates the ambiguity.

REVISION: The data show that the longer the enzyme was exposed to the salt solution, the lower the enzyme activity in the assay. Exposure to the salt solution may change the conformation of the enzyme, resulting in lower enzyme-substrate activity.

Another source of ambiguity is when a pronoun (him, her, it, he, she, its) could refer to two possible antecedents. In the following example, can you determine what the writer meant by *it*?

EXAMPLE: With time, salt changes the conformation of the enzyme, which makes *it* less reactive with the substrate.

If there is any doubt about what *it* refers to, replace *it* with the appropriate noun phrase.

REVISION: With time, salt changes the conformation of the enzyme, so that the enzyme can no longer react with its substrate.

Use connecting words and repetition to improve flow. A smooth transition from one sentence to the next is essential for reader comprehension. Consider the following example:

EXAMPLE: Catalase is an enzyme that breaks down hydrogen peroxide in both plant and animal cells. Low
or high temperature can lower the rate at which
the catalase can react with the hydrogen peroxide.
In optimal conditions, the enzyme functions at a
rate that will prevent any substantial buildup of
the toxin. If the temperature is too low, the rate
will be too slow, but high temperatures lead to
the denaturation of the enzyme.

Where is the writer going with this paragraph? The sentences do not seem
to flow, because there is no guidance from the writer on how one sentence
is related to the next. To improve flow, use connecting words such as *however, thus, although, in contrast, similarly, on the other hand, in addition to,* and
furthermore. Repetition of a key word from the previous sentence also helps
the reader make connections between sentences.

REVISION: Catalase is an enzyme that breaks down hydrogen
peroxide in both plant and animal cells. One of the
factors that affects the rate *of this reaction* is temperature. At optimal *temperatures,* the rate is sufficient
to prevent substantial buildup of the toxic hydrogen peroxide. If the temperature is too low, *however,*
the rate will be too slow, and hydrogen peroxide
accumulates in the cell. *On the other hand,* high temperatures may denature the enzyme.

6. Grammar

Grammar refers to the rules that deal with the form and structure of
words and their arrangement in sentences. This section describes three of
the most common offenses. See Hacker (1997), Lunsford (2001), or
Lunsford and Connors (1995, 1999) for a more comprehensive treatment
of the subject.

Make subjects and verbs agree.   We learn early on in our formal educa-
tion to make the verb agree with the subject. Most of us know that *the
sample was...,* but that *the samples were...* Most errors with subject-verb
agreement occur when there are words *between* the subject and the verb,
as in the following example.

EXAMPLE: *The samples* in the assay *were* [not was] incubated at
37°C for 10 min.

When you write complex sentences, ask yourself what is the subject of the sentence. Look for the verb that goes with that subject, and then mentally remove the words in between. Make the subject and its verb agree.

A second situation in which subject–verb agreement becomes confusing is when there are two subjects joined by *and*, as in the following example.

> **EXAMPLE:** An enzyme's amino acid *sequence and* its three-dimensional *structure make* [not makes] the enzyme-substrate relationship unique.

Compound subjects joined by *and* are almost always plural.

Write in complete sentences. A complete sentence consists of a subject and a verb. If the sentence starts with a subordinate word or words such as *after, although, because, before, but, if, so that, that, though, unless, until, when, where, who,* or *which,* however, another clause must complete the sentence.

> **EXAMPLE 1:** High temperatures destroy the three-dimensional structure of enzymes. Thus changing the effectiveness of the enzymes. [The second "sentence" is a fragment.]

> **REVISION:** High temperatures destroy the three-dimensional structure of enzymes, thus changing their effectiveness. [Combine the fragment with the previous sentence, changing punctuation as needed.]

> **EXAMPLE 2:** The standard curve for the Biuret assay was used to determine the protein concentration of the serial dilutions of the egg white. Although only those dilutions whose protein concentrations fell within the sensitivity range of the assay were multiplied by the dilution factor to give the original concentration of the egg white. [The second "sentence" is a fragment.]

> **REVISION:** The standard curve for the Biuret assay was used to determine the protein concentration of the serial dilutions of the egg white. Only those dilutions whose protein concentrations fell within the sensitivity range of the assay were multiplied by the dilution factor to give the

original concentration of the egg white. [Delete the subordinate word(s) to make a complete sentence.]

Revise run-on sentences. Run-on sentences consist of two or more independent clauses joined without proper punctuation. Each independent clause could stand alone as a complete sentence. Run-on sentences are common in first drafts, where your main objective is to get your ideas down on paper (or electronic media, if you use a computer). When you revise your first draft, however, use one of the following strategies to revise run-on sentences:

- Insert a comma and a coordinating conjunction (*and, but, or, nor, for, so,* or *yet*).
- Use a semicolon or possibly a colon.
- Make two separate sentences.
- Rewrite the sentence.

EXAMPLE 1: The class data for the Bradford method were scattered, those for the Biuret method were closer.

REVISION A: The class data for the Bradford method were scattered, but those for the Biuret method were closer. [Use a coordinating conjunction.]

REVISION B: The class data for the Bradford method were scattered; those for the Biuret method were closer. [Use a semicolon.]

EXAMPLE 2: The readings from the spectrophotometer should show a correlation between protein concentration and absorbance, this is Beer's law, which relates absorbance to the path length of light along with molar concentration of a solute and the molar coefficient. [Fused sentence]

REVISION A: The readings from the spectrophotometer should show a correlation between protein concentration and absorbance; this is Beer's law, which relates absorbance to the path length of light along with molar concentration of a solute and the molar coefficient. [Use a semicolon to separate the two clauses.]

REVISION B: The readings from the spectrophotometer should show a correlation between protein concentration and absorbance. This relationship is described by Beer's law, which relates absorbance to the path length of light along with molar concentration of a solute and the molar coefficient. [Make two separate sentences.]

EXAMPLE 3:   An increase in enzyme concentration increased the reaction rate as did an increase in substrate concentration, so the concentrations of the molecules have an influence on how the enzyme reacts.

REVISION A: As enzyme concentration and substrate concentration increased, so did the reaction rate. [Rewrite the sentence. The second half of the original sentence was deleted because it is deadwood.]

REVISION B: Enzyme and substrate concentration influence enzyme reaction rate: an increase in enzyme or substrate concentration increased reaction rate. [Use a colon.]

7. Word usage

When you write the right words in the right situations, readers have confidence in your work. Use a standard dictionary whenever you are not sure about word usage. Consult your textbook and laboratory exercise for proper spelling and usage of technical terms. The following word pairs are frequently confused in students' biology papers.

absorbance, absorbency, observance   *Absorbance* is how much light a solution absorbs; absorbance is measured with a spectrophotometer. *According to Beer's law, absorbance is proportional to* *concentration. Absorbency* is how much moisture a diaper or paper towel can hold. *Brand A paper towels show greater absorbency than Brand B paper towels. Observance* is the act of observing. *Government offices are closed today in observance of Independence Day.*

affect, effect   *Affect* is a verb that means "to influence." Affect is never used as a noun. *Temperature affects enzyme activity. Effect* can be used either as a noun or a verb. When used as a noun, *effect* means "result." *We studied the effect of temperature on enzyme activity.* When used as a verb, effect means "to cause." *High temperature effected a change in enzyme conformation, which destroyed enzyme activity.*

alga, algae   See Plurals.

amount, number   Use *amount* when the quantity cannot be counted. *The reaction rate depends on the amount of enzyme in the solution.* Use *number* if you can count individual pieces. *The reaction rate depends on the number of enzyme molecules in the solution.*

analysis, analyses   See Plurals.

bacterium, bacteria   See Plurals.

bind, bond   *Bind* is a verb meaning "to link." *The active site is the region of an enzyme where a substrate binds. Bond* is a noun that refers to the chemical linkage between atoms. *Proteins consist of amino acids joined by peptide bonds. Bond* used as a verb means "to stick together." *This 5-minute epoxy glue can be used to bond hard plastic.*

complementary, complimentary   *Complementary* means "something needed to complete;" matching. *The DNA double helix consists of complementary base pairs: A always pairs with T, and G with C. Complimentary* means "given free as a courtesy." *The brochures at the Visitor's Center are complimentary.*

confirmation, conformation   *Confirmation* means "verification." *I received confirmation from the postal service that my package had arrived. Conformation* is the three-dimensional structure of a macromolecule. *Noncovalent bonds help maintain a protein's stable conformation.*

continual, continuous   *Continual* means "going on repeatedly and frequently over a period of time." *The continual chatter of a group of inconsiderate students during the lecture annoyed me. Continuous* means "going on without interruption over a period of time." *The bacteria were grown in L-broth continuously for 48 hr.*

create, prepare, produce   *Create* is to cause to come into existence. *The artist used wood and plastic to create this sculpture. Prepare* means "to make ready." *The protein standards were prepared from a 50 mg/mL stock solution. Produce* means to make or manufacture. *The reaction between hydrogen peroxide and catalase produces water and oxygen.*

datum, data   See Plurals.

different, differing   *Different* is an adjective that means "not alike." An adjective modifies a noun. *Different concentrations of bovine serum albumin were prepared. Differing* is the intransitive tense of "to differ," a verb that means "to vary." It is incorrect to replace the word *different* with *differing* in the preceding example, because *differing* implies that a single concentration changes depending on time or circumstance. This situation is highly unlikely with bovine serum albumin, which is quite stable under laboratory conditions! An acceptable use of *differing* is shown in the following example. *Bovine serum albumin solutions, differing in their protein content, were prepared.*

effect, affect   See affect, effect.

fewer, less   Use *fewer* when the quantity can be counted. *The reaction rate was lower, because there were fewer collisions between enzyme and substrate molecules.* Use *less* when the quantity cannot be counted. *The weight of this sample was less than I expected.*

formula, formulas, formulae   See Plurals.

hypothesis, hypotheses   See Plurals.

its, it's   *Its* is a possessive pronoun meaning "belonging to it." *The Bradford assay is preferred because of its greater sensitivity. It's* is a contraction of "it is." *The Bradford assay is preferred because* *it's more sensitive.* (**Note:** **Contractions should not be used in formal writing.**)

less, fewer   See fewer, less

lose, loose   *Lose* means to misplace or fail to maintain something. *An enzyme may lose its effectiveness at high temperatures. Loose* means "not tight." *When you autoclave solutions, make sure the lid on the bottle is loose.*

lowered, raised   Both of these are transitive verbs, which means that they require a direct object (a noun to act on). **Wrong**: *The fish's body temperature lowered in response to the cold water.* **Right**: *The cold water lowered the fish's body temperature.*

medium, media   See Plurals.

observance   See absorbance, absorbency, observance.

phenomenon, phenomena   See Plurals.

Plurals   The plural and singular forms of some words used in biology are given in Table 5.4. A common mistake with these words is failure to make the subject and verb agree. Some disciplines treat *data* as singular, but scientists and engineers subscribe to the strict interpretation that *data* is plural. The data *show…* [not *shows*] is correct.

prepare   See create, prepare, produce.

produce   See create, prepare, produce.

raised, lowered   See lowered, raised.

ratio, ration   *Ratio* is a proportion or quotient. *The ratio of protein in the final dilution was 1:5. Ration* is a fixed portion, often referring to food. *The Red Cross distributed rations to the refugees.*

strain, strand   A *strain* is a line of individuals of a certain species, usually distinguished by some special characteristic. *The*

TABLE 5.4 Singular and plural of some common biological words

SINGULAR	PLURAL
alga	algae
analysis	analyses
bacterium	bacteria
criterion	criteria
datum (rarely used)	data
formula	formulas, formulae
hypothesis	hypotheses
index	indexes, indices
medium	media
phenomenon	phenomena
ratio	ratios

lacI⁻ strain of E. coli produces a nonfunctional repressor protein. A strand is a ropelike length of something. *The strands of DNA are held together with hydrogen bonds.*

that, which   Use *that* with restrictive clauses. A restrictive clause limits the reference to a certain group. Use *which* with nonrestrictive clauses. A nonrestrictive clause does not limit the reference, but rather provides additional information. Commas are used to set off nonrestrictive clauses but not restrictive clauses. Consider the following examples:

EXAMPLE 1:   The Bradford assay, which is one method for measuring protein concentration, requires only a small amount of sample. [*Which* begins a phrase that provides additional information, but is not essential to make a complete sentence.]

EXAMPLE 2:   Enzyme activity decreased significantly, which suggests that the enzyme was denatured at 50°C. [*Which* refers to the entire phrase *Enzyme activity decreased significantly,* not to any specific element.]

EXAMPLE 3:   The samples that had high absorbance readings were diluted. [*That* refers specifically to *The samples.*]

than, then   *Than* is an expression used to compare two things. *Collisions between molecules occur more frequently at high temperatures than at low temperatures. Then* means "next in time." *First 1 mL of protein sample was added to the text tube. Then 4 mL of Biuret reagent was added.*

various, varying   *Various* is an adjective that means "different." *Various hypotheses were proposed to explain the observations. Varying* is a verb that means "changing." *Varying the substrate concentration while keeping the enzyme concentration constant allows you to determine the effect of substrate concentration on enzyme activity.* Analogous to *different, differing,* replacing the word *various* with *varying* in the preceding example changes the meaning of the sentence. *Varying* implies that a single hypothesis changes depending on time or circumstance. *Various* implies that different hypotheses were proposed.

8. Spelling

Spell checkers in word processing programs are so easy to use that there is really no excuse for *not* using them. Just remember that spell checkers may not know scientific terminology, so consult your textbook or laboratory manual for correct spelling. In some cases, the spell checker may even try to get you to change a properly used scientific word to an inappropriate word that happens to be in its database (for example, *absorbance* to *absorbency*).

The following poem is an example of how indiscriminate use of the spell checker can produce garbage:

Wrest a Spell

Eye halve a spelling chequer
It came with my pea sea
It plainly marques four my revue
Miss steaks eye kin knot sea.

Eye strike a key and type a word
And weight four it two say
Weather eye am wrong oar write
It shows me strait a weigh.

As soon as a mist ache is maid
It nose bee fore two long
And eye can put the error rite
Its rare lea ever wrong.

Eye have run this poem threw it
I am shore your pleased two no
Its letter perfect awl the weigh
My chequer tolled me sew.

— Sauce unknown

Spell checkers will also not catch mistakes of usage, for example *form* if
you really meant *from*. Print out your document and proofread the hard
copy carefully.

9. Global Revision

Organization. Is your document formatted according to "Instructions to
Authors"? Is your scientific paper divided into sections? Does each section
have the right content? The "Biology Lab Report Checklist" (pp. 92–93) and
"Laboratory Report Mistakes" (pp. 104–107) tables can alert you to poten-
tial problem areas.

Content. Is your paper focussed on the subject? Did you provide all of the
necessary supporting materials (tables and figures) to support your conclusions? Did you answer all of the questions in the laboratory exercise?
Use the "Biology Lab Report Checklist" and "Laboratory Report Mistakes"
key.

Style. Read your paper aloud. Listen for awkward sentence structure and illogical reasoning. Avoid wordiness and flowery language that might make your meaning ambiguous. Use definite and specific sentences. Keep related words together. Consider the following sentence taken from an English-language newspaper in Japan: "A committee was formed to examine brain death in the Prime Minister's office." Although brain death in the Prime Minister's office may be a political reality, what was really intended was "A committee was formed in the Prime Minister's office to examine brain death."

Focus on the following to achieve a clear and readable style.

a. Paragraphs
   - Each paragraph focuses on one topic.
   - First sentence introduces the topic.
   - Subsequent sentences support the topic sentence.
   - Connecting phrases are used to achieve good flow between sentences.

b. Sentences
   - Eliminate wordiness.
   - Vary sentence structure and length to avoid monotony.
   - Use punctuation correctly.
   - Use passive and active voice appropriately.
   - Use past and present tense appropriately.

c. Words and phrases
   - Make them concise and descriptive.
   - Use scientific words when appropriate. Define terms that might be unfamiliar to your audience. Avoid jargon and anthropomorphism, and teleological arguments.
   - Watch out for commonly confused word pairs such as *effect* and *affect*, *it's* and *its*, *then* and *than*, and others.
   - Avoid clichés, slang, and sexist language.
   - Do not use contractions in formal writing.

TITLE (p. 55–56)

☐ Descriptive and concise

AUTHORS

☐ Writer is first author, lab partner(s) second (third, etc.) author

ABSTRACT (pp. 54–55)

☐ Contains purpose of experiment
☐ Contains brief description of methods
☐ Contains results
☐ Contains conclusions

INTRODUCTION (pp. 53–54)

☐ The rationale is included. Hypotheses are clearly stated.
☐ Contains background information from the literature (primary references)
☐ Selected references are directly relevant to your experiment.
☐ Citation format is correct.
☐ Citations are paraphrased. Direct quotations are not used.
☐ Objectives of experiment are clearly stated.

MATERIALS AND METHODS (pp. 32–36)

☐ Contains all relevant information to enable the reader to repeat the experiment. This includes volumes, temperatures, wavelengths, and so on (p. 35).
☐ Citation format is correct.
☐ Materials are not listed separately (p. 33)
☐ No references to containers (pp. 33–34)
☐ No preview of how the data will be organized or interpreted (p. 35)
☐ Written in paragraph form (not a numbered list) (p. 33)
☐ Written in past tense (p. 33)

Biology Lab Report Checklist

RESULTS (pp. 36–51)

☐ Results of statistical analyses are stated.

☐ Figures and tables are present. Figure captions go below figure; table captions go above table (pp. 40–46)

☐ Text is present. Reference is made to each table and figure, and the results are described in words (pp. 37–39).

☐ Figure and table titles are informative and can be understood apart from the text (pp. 40–43).

☐ No explanation is given for the results (p. 36).

DISCUSSION (p. 53)

☐ All conclusions are supported by data or citations.

☐ Results are briefly summarized as explanations are given; implications are considered.

☐ Errors and inconsistencies are pointed out.

REFERENCES (pp. 56–62)

☐ References consist mostly of primary journal articles, not textbooks or Internet sources.

☐ Reference format is correct and complete.

☐ All references have been cited in the text. All citations in the text have been included in the References section.

REVISION

☐ Conventions in biology (pp. 66–69)

☐ Numbers (pp. 69–70)

☐ Standard abbreviations (pp. 70, 72–73)

☐ Punctuation (pp. 70–71, 74–76)

☐ Clarity (pp. 77–81)

☐ Grammar (pp. 81–84)

☐ Word usage (pp. 84–89)

☐ Spelling (pp. 89–90)

☐ Global revision (pp. 90–91)

☐ All questions from the laboratory exercise have been answered

Biology Lab Report Checklist

Chapter 6

A "Good" Sample Student Laboratory Report

The laboratory report in this chapter was written by Lynne Waldman during her first year at Bucknell University, in an introductory course for biology majors. Lynne and her lab partners designed and carried out an original project in which they investigated the effect of a fungus on the growth of bean, pea, and corn plants.

Lynne's report has many of the characteristics of a well-written scientific paper. When you look over her presentation, notice the style and tone of her writing, as well as the format of the paper. The comments and annotations alert you to important points to keep in mind when you write your laboratory report.

The presentation here has been typeset to fit this book and to accommodate the annotations. Your report should be formatted to fit standard $8\frac{1}{2} \times 11$ inch paper. Unless you are instructed otherwise, use a serif type (Times Roman is standard), double space, and leave 1 inch of margin all around.

For details on how to format documents in Microsoft Word, see Appendix 1.

The Effects of the Fungus *Phytophthora infestans* on Bean, Pea, and Corn Plants

Lynne Waldman, Partner One, Partner Two

Informative title

Author's name first, followed by lab partners' names in alphabetical order

Sections of report are clearly labeled.

Background information is present.

No references are used in Abstract.

Purpose of current experiment is given.

Short description of methods

Results are given.

No references are made to figures.

Short explanation of results is given.

Abstract is a maximum of 250 words long.

Background information

Latin names are italicized.

Abstract

Phytophthora infestans is a fast-spreading, parasitic fungus that caused the infamous potato blight by devastating Ireland's crops in the 1840s. *P. infestans* also causes late blight in tomato plants, a relative of the potato. In this experiment, the effects of *P. infestans* on *Phaseolus* variety long bush bean, *Zea mays* (corn), and *Pisum sativum* (pea) were studied. The soil surrounding the roots of 18-day old plants was injected with *P. infestans* cultured in an L-broth medium. Plant height, number of leaves, and leaf angle were measured for each plant during the next 8 days. Chlorophyll assays were performed prior to exposure, and on the eighth day after exposure to the fungus. The plants were also examined for black or brown leaf spots characteristic of late blight infections. The results showed that *P. infestans* had no apparent effect on the bean, corn, and pea plants. One reason for this may be that there were no fungus zoospores in the L-broth medium. More probably, however, *P. infestans* may be a species-specific pathogen that cannot infect bean, corn, or pea plants.

Introduction

Originating in Peruvian-Bolivian Andes, the potato *(Solanum tuberosum)* is one of the world's four most important food crops (along with wheat, rice, and corn). Cultivation of potatoes began in South America over 1,800 years ago, and through the Spanish conquistadors, the tuber was introduced into Europe in the second half of the 1600s. By the beginning of the 18th century, the potato was widely grown in Ireland, and the country's economy heavily relied on the potato crop. In the middle of the 19th century, Ireland's potato crop suffered widespread late blight disease caused by *Phytophthora infestans,* a species of pathogenic plant fungus. Failure of the potato crop because of late blight resulted in the Irish potato famine. The famine led to widespread starvation and the death of about a million Irish.

The potato continues to be one of the world's main food crops. However, *P. infestans* has reemerged in a chemical-resistant form in the United States, Canada, Mexico, and Europe (McElreath, 1994). Late blight caused by the new strains is costing growers world-wide about $3 billion annually. The need to apply chemical fungicides eight to ten times a season further increases the cost to the grower (Stanley, 1994 and Stanley, 1997). *P. infestans* is thus an economically important pathogen.

Proper citation format is used (Name-Year system).

No direct quotations are used. Citations are paraphrased and the source is given in parentheses.

P. infestans, which can destroy a potato crop in the field or in storage, thrives in warm, damp weather. The parasitic fungus causes black or purple lesions on a potato plant's stem and leaves. As a result of infection by this fungus, the plant is unable to photosynthesize, develops a slimy rot, and dies. *P. infestans* similarly infects the tomato plant *(Lycopersicon esculentum).*

The purpose of the present experiment was to determine the effects of *P. infestans* on plant height, number of leaves, leaf angle, and chlorophyll content of three agriculturally important plants: *Phaseolus* variety long bush beans, *Zea mays* (corn), and *Pisum sativum* (peas). Symptoms of fungal infection were assumed to be similar to that in potatoes.

Purpose of experiment is clearly stated.

Materials and Methods
Phaseolus variety long bush bean, *Zea mays* (corn) and *Pisum sativum* (pea) seeds were soaked overnight in tap water. Fifteen randomly chosen seeds of each species were planted 1 cm beneath the surface in three separate trays containing 10 cm of potting soil. Another set of trays, which was to be the control group, was prepared in the same fashion. All the experimental plants were placed in one fume hood, and all the control plants were placed in

M&M are always written in past tense.

Sufficient detail is given to allow the reader to repeat the experiment.

relative positions in another fume hood in the same room. The plants were exposed to the ambient light intensity in the hood (153 fc) and air current 24 hrs a day, and were watered lightly daily. The plants were allowed to germinate and grow for 18 days.

Phytophthora infestans on potato dextrose agar was obtained from Carolina Biological Supply House. At day 10 of the plant growth regime, pieces of agar on which the fungus was growing were transferred to L-broth. L-broth consisted of 5 g yeast extract, 10 g tryptone, 1 g dextrose, and 10 g NaCl dissolved in distilled water, and adjusted to pH 7.1, to make 1 L of medium. The medium was sterilized before adding the fungal culture. After 4 days in L-broth, 6 mL of the fungal culture was injected into the soil around the roots of each 18-day old plant. 6 mL of L-broth without *P. infestans* was injected into the soil of the control plants. All plants were then allowed to grow for another 8 days.

Every other day after treatment with *P. infestans*, plant height and number of leaves were measured for both the control and the experimental plants. Plant height was measured from the soil to the apical meristem of the plant. Leaf angle (as shown in Figure 1) of the largest, lowest leaf on each plant was measured three times, once prior to injection, once 4 days after injection, and once 8 days after injection. Leaf angle was measured in order to determine if *P. infestans* causes wilting in the three plant

Figures that explain the methodology may be included in M&M section.

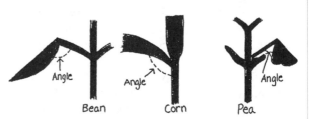

Figure 1 Leaf angle as measured in bean, corn, and pea plants

species. In addition, the plant was examined visually for the presence of any leaf spots.

Chlorophyll assays were performed on one plant from each tray prior to injection and on the eighth day after injection. For each chlorophyll assay, the leaves of the plant were removed from the stem. For each 0.1 g of leaves, 6.0 mL of 100% methanol were used. The leaves were thoroughly ground in half of the methanol with a pestle in a mortar. The leaves were ground again after the rest of the methanol was added. Extraction of the chlorophyll was allowed to proceed for 45 min at room temperature. Then the suspension was gravity filtered through filter paper to remove the leaf parts. The absorbance of the filtrate was measured with a Spectronic 20 spectrophotometer at 652 nm and 665.2 nm. The absorbance values were converted to relative chlorophyll units using the following equation derived by Porra and colleagues (1989):

Total chlorophyll (a and b) = Dilution factor $\times$ [22.12 $A_{652\ nm}$ + 2.71$A_{665.2\ nm}$ (mg/L)] $\times$ Volume of solvent (L) / Weight of leaves (mg)

Subscripts are made properly.

Results

P. infestans-treated plants and the control plants had similar growth patterns (Figure 2). Both the experimental and control pea and corn plants grew at a constant, but very slow rate over the eight day test peri-

Results section must contain a text in which the author presents each figure and table to the reader.

Reference is made to the next figure in the sequence, and the important results are described.

Figure is large enough to read key and axes easily.

Axes have proper spacing.

Figure 2 Average height of control and experimental plants in the period after injection with *P. infestans*

Points and lines on curve are dark and can be easily distinguished from each other.

Units are given in parentheses after the axis label (where applicable).

Figure caption is located below figure.

Figure title is not simply a repeat of "*y*-axis label vs. *x*-axis label ."

Figure number sequence is correct.

Reference is made to the next figure and the important information is described.

Symbols (such as °) are typed using word processing software.

Figure 3 Average number of leaves of control and experimental plants in the period after injection with *P. infestans*

od. The control bean plants were taller on average than the experimental bean plants throughout most of the experiment. Both groups showed the same growth pattern, however, with rapid growth occurring from day 18 to 24 (0 to 4 days after injection), followed by slower growth to the end of the experiment.

As plant height increased, the average number of leaves on all of the plants also increased over the measurement period (Figure 3). There is an uncharacteristic decrease in the number of leaves of pea plants treated with *P. infestans* from day 18 to 20 (0 to 2 days after injection), but this is probably due to counting error.

There was a general decline in average leaf angle of all the plants over the first four days after injection with *P. infestans* (Figure 4). The plants did not follow this pattern over the second half of the experiment, however. The leaf angle of the experimental bean group increased by 28°, while that of the control bean group only increased by about 3°. The leaf angle of the control pea plants increased significantly (33°), while that of the experimental pea plants decreased 4°. The leaf angle of the corn control group decreased 0.5°, while that of the corn experimental group showed a much sharper decline of 24°.

There was also no difference between the experimental and control groups with regard to chlorophyll content. There was a slight increase in chlorophyll

Figure 4 Average leaf angle of control and experimental plants in the period after injection with *P. infestans*

content from day 18 to 26 (0 to 8 days after injection) in the corn plants (Table 1). For the bean group, there was a large decrease in chlorophyll content, 0.1 relative chlorophyll units, which did not seem to agree with the general appearance of the plants. There may have been some error when this assay was carried out. There was little change in chlorophyll content for the pea group.

Table is numbered properly.

Finally, there was no evidence of any brown or black leaf spots symptomatic of *P. infestans* infection.

Discussion

Table 1 Chlorophyll content of corn, bean, and pea plants prior to infection and 8 days after infection

Table caption is placed above the table.

Plant	Relative chlorophyll units		Change in chlorophyll content (relative units)
Plant	Day 0	Day 8	
Corn, treated	9.036×10^{-4}	9.383×10^{-4}	$+3.45 \times 10^{-5}$
Corn, control	9.270×10^{-4}	8.963×10^{-4}	$+3.34 \times 10^{-5}$
Bean, treated	1.034×10^{-1}	1.2×10^{-3}	-1.022×10^{-1}
Bean, control	1.7×10^{-3}	1.6×10^{-3}	-1×10^{-4}
Pea, treated	1.3×10^{-3}	1.7×10^{-3}	$+4 \times 10^{-4}$
Pea, control	1.2×10^{-3}	1.2×10^{-3}	0.0000

Scientific notation is used correctly.

It is preferable to leave extra space at the bottom of the page, rather than to split a table across a page.

Results are summarized
or briefly restated in the
Discussion section.

Explanations for
results are given.

References are used to
support explanations.

Ways to test
explanations may
be offered.

Frequent use of
references is made to
support explanations.
Whenever possible, use
primary references
(journal articles,
conference proceedings,
collections of primary
articles in a book). Avoid
textbooks (secondary
references) and Internet
sources (may be
unreliable).

P. infestans did not affect the plant height, leaf angle, number of leaves, and chlorophyll content of *Zea mays, Pisum sativum,* or *Phaseolus.* Symptoms of infection are the presence of brown or black spots (areas of dead tissue) on leaves and stems, and, as the infection spreads, the entire plant becomes covered with a cottony film (Stanley, 1994). None of the experimental plants exhibited these symptoms.

There may be several reasons why *P. infestans* did not affect the plants in this study. One reason is that the L-broth culture of *P. infestans* may not have contained zoospores of the fungus. Zoospores are motile spores that can penetrate the host plant through the leaves and soft shoots, or through the roots (Stanley, 1994). Zoospores are usually produced in wet, warm weather conditions (Ingold and Hudson, 1993). If the L-broth culture did not contain any zoospores, or if the soil around the plants was not sufficiently saturated to stimulate production of zoospores, then these conditions may have prevented *P. infestans* from attacking the roots and shoots of the plants.

In order to determine if the problem was lack of zoospores, first the L-broth culture could be examined microscopically for presence of zoospores. Second, the *P. infestans* plants could be watered with different quantities of water to determine if the fungus requires wetter soil for zoospore production and motility.

Another reason why *P. infestans* may not have affected the plants is that this species of fungus may be specific to potato *(Solanum tuberosum)* and tomato *(Lycopersicon esculentum)* plants (Stanley, 1994), which both belong to the nightshade family (Solanaceae). In contrast, corn belongs to the grass family (Gramineae), and peas and beans are legumes (Leguminosae). It may be that these plant families are not susceptible to *P. infestans*, which has a very limited host range (Stanley, 1994). Non-susceptible plants have been shown to have defense mechanisms that prevent *P. infestans* from infecting them (Gallegly, 1995).

Further research is required to determine if *P. infestans* really cannot infect corn, pea, and bean plants. Goth and Keane (1997) developed a test to measure resistance of potato and tomato varieties to original and new strains of *P. infestans*. Their experiments involved exposing the experimental plants' leaves directly to the fungus, and this method could perhaps be tested on corn, pea, and bean leaves as well.

References

Gallegly ME. 1995. New criteria for classifying Phytophthora and critique of existing approaches. In: Erwin DC, Bartnicki-Garcia S, Tsao PH, editors. Phytophthora: Its Biology, Taxonomy, Ecology, and Pathology St. Paul: The American Phytopathological Society. pp. 167–172.

Goth RW and Keane J. 1997. A detached-leaf method to evaluate late blight resistance in potato and tomato. Am. J. Potato Res. 74(5): 347–352.

Ingold CT and Hudson HJ. 1993. The Biology of Fungi, 6th ed. London: Chapman and Hall.

McElreath, Linda R. 1994. One potato, two potato. J. Agri. Research 42(5): 2–3.

Porra RJ., Thompson WA and Kriedemann PE. 1989. Determination of accurate extinction coefficients and simultaneous equations for assaying chlorophylls a and b extracted with four different solvents: verification of the concentration of chlorophyll standards by atomic absorption spectroscopy. Biochim. Biophys. Acta 975: 384–394.

Stanley D. 1994. What was around comes around. Agricultural Research 42(5): 4–8.

Stanley D. 1997. Potatoes. J. Agri. Research 45(5): 10–14.

When Name-Year citation format is used, authors are listed alphabetically in the References section.

Most references should be primary journal articles or articles in books. Textbooks and articles in newspapers and magazines are secondary references (less preferable).

List all authors (up to 10; then list first 10 followed by "et al.")

See the tabbed pages in Chapter 4 for examples of how to reference journal articles, articles in books, and books.

List the starting and ending pages of the article, not just the page(s) you extracted information from.

All citations must have a corresponding reference.

All references must be cited in the text.

Laboratory Report Mistakes

The following table lists some common mistakes made by students writing biology lab reports. When you proofread the first draft of your report, look over this list and be on the lookout for these kinds of mistakes.

Your instructor may also use this key to save time grading lab reports without sacrificing the quality of the feedback. For example, the number "8" written in the left margin means that you failed to include essential information in the Abstract. If your instructor uses this system, be sure to refer to the key for an explanation of your instructor's comments.

Although some of these mistakes may not affect the content of your paper, they do affect your credibility as a scientist; careless writing may be equated with careless science.

MISTAKE	EXPLANATION
lc	Use lowercase letter
CAP or uc	Use capital (uppercase) letter
^	Insert text
⌒	Leave space between the two characters
⌒⌄	Close up
¶	Start a new paragraph
Page break	End the current page; move subsequent text to next page. (In Microsoft Word and WordPerfect, press Ctrl + Enter where you want to end the page.)
agr	Subject and verb do not agree.
wc	Word choice. Word used is not appropriate for the situation.
. . . . . .	A dotted underline means "stet," or "let original text stand." The correction was made in error.
1	Word usage incorrect. Look it up in the dictionary. Examples:
a.	absorbance (how much light is absorbed) vs. absorbency (how much moisture a diaper or paper towel can hold)
b.	to bind (what atoms and molecules do) vs. to bond (what glue does)
c.	complementary (DNA strands) vs. complimentary (given free as a courtesy)
d.	data = plural of "datum"; e.g. "These data show…" *not* "This data shows…"

e.	effect (noun) vs. effect (verb meaning "to cause") vs. affect (verb meaning "to influence")
f.	conformation (3-D shape of a protein) vs. confirmation (verification)
i.	it's (it is) vs. its (belonging to "it")
m.	amount (cannot count individual pieces) vs. number (can count individual pieces)
r.	ratio (proportion or quotient) vs. ration (a fixed portion of food)
s.	strain of bacteria vs. strand of DNA
t.	then (next in time) vs. than (an expression for comparing two things)
v.	varying (changing) vs. various (different)
2	Latin names should be *italicized.*
3	Write in passive voice. Shift the emphasis from yourself to the subject of the action.
4	Punctuation usage is incorrect.
5	Sentence structure is awkward or sentence is incomplete.
6	Symbols should not be handwritten.
7	Superscript/Subscript. Superscript: For 10^{-5}, for example, this is done by first typing "10–5"; then highlight "–5" and either click the Superscript button on the toolbar or select the formatting function from your word processor. Subscript: For K_m, for example, this is done by first typing "*Km*"; then highlight "*m*" and either click the Subscript button on the toolbar or select or select the formatting function from your word processor.
8	Essential Abstract content is missing. Abstract must contain purpose, brief description of methods, results, and conclusions or possible explanation for the results.
9	Too much detail for Abstract.
10	Introduction needs references to provide background.
11	Introduction needs purpose of the current experiment.
12	Wrong citation format. Use either name-year or citation-sequence format. See Chapter 4 for specific examples.
13	Do not use direct quotations in scientific writing. Paraphrase and cite the source.

Laboratory Report Mistakes

14	Write Materials and Methods in paragraph form. Do not make a numbered list.
15	Do not list materials separately in Materials and Methods section, unless the source is noncommercial or critical for the outcome of the experiment.
16	Time frame does not affect the outcome.
17	Do not refer to the container; instead emphasize the contents and give appropriate units of concentration.
18	Do not describe routine laboratory procedures in detail.
19	In the Materials and Methods section, do not give a "preview" of how data will be organized in the Results section.
20	Essential details are missing in the Materials and Methods section. Provide enough detail to enable the reader to repeat the experiment.
21	Do not include raw data in the Results section; instead, summarize and organize the data.
22	Results section always needs a text.
23	Describe *each* table and *each* figure individually and sequentially.
24	Refer to each figure/table parenthetically by number as you describe the results.
25	A table is not needed when the figure(s) shows the same data.
26	Each figure/table must have a number and a title.
27	The figure/table title must be self-explanatory without reference to the text.
28	Uninformative figure title. Do not use "y-axis label vs. x-axis label" as a title. See Chapter 4 for examples.
29	Figure caption goes *below* figure; table caption goes *above* table.
30	No title is needed above the figure. When you make the figure in Excel, leave the "Chart title" space blank.
31	Axis does not have proper spacing. Choose "XY Scatter" plot in Excel (see Appendix 2).
32	Each data set must have its own distinguishable symbols or lines. Choose a dark color for both the line and the symbol.
33	Use scientific notation when numbers are very large or very small.
34	Units are needed.

35	Number format is incorrect. Do not start sentences with a number (write out the number). Make sure decimal numbers less than one start with zero, e.g. 0.1 mL, *not* .1 mL.
36	Discussion section requires an explanation of the results.
37	Discussion section requires a comparison of your data to what is known from the literature. Science is not done in a vacuum!
38	Wrong reference format. See Chapter 4 for specific examples.
39	All citations in the text must be listed in the References section.
40	All references must be cited in the text.

Laboratory Report Mistakes

Chapter 7

POSTER PRESENTATIONS

Posters are a means of communicating research results quickly. They provide a great opportunity to get feedback about preliminary data and ideas. **Poster sessions** are often held at large national meetings, and they allow you to meet other scientists in an informal setting.

Why Posters?

Scientists who attend poster sessions constitute a much larger audience than the one attracted to a journal article on a particular topic. Thus, your goal is to produce a poster that not only attracts experts in your subdiscipline, but also the much larger group of scientists with tangential research interests. The latter group provides a unique opportunity for you to learn about applications of your work to other research areas (and vice versa), spurs scientific creativity, and prompts you to apply an interdisciplinary approach to problem-solving.

An appropriate poster presentation should fulfill two objectives. First, it must be aesthetically pleasing to attract viewers in the first place. Second, it must communicate the methods, results, and conclusions clearly and concisely.

Poster Content

Posters are *not* papers; they rely more on visuals than on text to present the message. It is not necessary to supply as many supporting details as you would for a paper, because you (the author) will be present to discuss details one-on-one with interested individuals. Too much material may even discourage individuals from reading your poster.

Posters presented at large national meetings should be organized so that readers can stand at least 10 feet away from the poster and get the take-home message in 30 seconds or less. Because of the large number of sessions (lectures) and an even larger number of posters, conference participants often experience "sensory overload." Thus, if you want your poster to stand out, make the section headings descriptive, the content brief and to the point, and the conclusions assertive and clear.

Posters for a student audience in the context of an in-house presentation should follow the same principle of brevity, but may retain the sections traditionally found in scientific papers. These include:

1. Title banner
2. Abstract
3. Introduction
4. Materials and Methods
5. Results
6. Discussion or Conclusions
7. References (these should be brief or omitted on the poster and provided on a handout)

1. Title Banner

Use a short, yet descriptive, title. This is the first and most important section for attracting viewers, so try to incorporate your most important conclusion in the title. For example, **Gibberellic Acid Makes Dwarf *B. rapa* Grow Taller** is more effective than **Effect of Gibberellic Acid on Dwarf *B. rapa*.**

The title banner should be at the top of the poster and in 72 point bold font, mixed type, or all caps, 65 characters or less on a line. Underneath the title, include the authors' names, in order of contribution, and the institutional affiliation(s). The authors of a scientific work have intellectual responsibility for the data and conclusions. Typically, the first author contributes the greatest effort to the work and the last author is the primary (or principle) investigator, or the scientist that is in charge of the lab and its funding. Use 48 point bold, mixed type for the authors' names.

2. Abstract

Optional – if present, it is a summary of the work presented in the poster.

3. Introduction

Instead of this conventional heading, consider using a short statement of the topic or introduce the topic as a question. Under the heading, briefly explain the existing state of knowledge of the topic, the rationale for the study, and what specifically you intended to demonstrate. A bulleted list of objectives may be a good way to present some of this information.

4. Materials and Methods

Present the methods you used to investigate the problem in enough detail so that someone competent in basic laboratory techniques could repeat your experiments. You might write the basic approach as a series of bulleted statements, and then provide more details in the subsequent text. Be both *brief* and *thorough*.

5. Results

The Results section of a poster consists mostly of visuals (pictures, tables, and graphs) and a minimum of text. Poster viewers do not have time to read the results leisurely, as they do with a journal article. An effective presentation of the results should announce each result with a heading, provide a visual that supports the result, and use text sparingly as a supplement to the visuals.

Figures are a summary of the raw data and are constructed so that viewers can appreciate both the general patterns of the data and the degree of variability that they possess. Written text should concentrate on general patterns, trends, and differences in the results, and not on the numbers themselves. For example, the reader can visualize "the concentration of chlorophyll increased initially, and then leveled off after 10 days" much more easily than "the chlorophyll concentration was 9×10^{-5} units on the fourth day, increased to 6×10^{-4} units on the tenth day, and then stayed about the same at 4×10^{-4} units on day 21."

Avoid using tables with large amounts of data; if you think the data are important, prepare the table to give as a handout. Your job is to sort through the data and come up with the take-home message. Do not use flip-out charts, in which one table or figure is displayed beneath another.

Figures may contain some statistical information including means and standard error and minimum and maximum values, where appropriate. Make the data points prominent and use a simple vertical line without crossbars for the error bars. Use the same sized font for the axis labels and the key as you use for the text (24 pt). Do not present the same data in both a table and as a figure.

Visuals in posters do not need a caption (number and title). Instead, the graphs and pictures are integrated so that they immediately follow the text in which they are first described.

Edit the text ruthlessly to remove nonessential information about the visuals. A sentence like "The effect of gibberellic acid on *B. rapa* is shown in the following figure." is nothing but deadwood. On the other hand, "*B. rapa* plants treated with gibberellic acid grew taller than those receiving only water" informs the reader of the result.

Remember to leave room for blank space on a poster. Space can be used to separate sections and gives the eyes a rest.

6. Discussion or Conclusions

Interpret the data in relation to the original objective or hypothesis and relate these interpretations to the present state of knowledge presented in the Introduction. Discuss any surprising results. Discuss the future needs or direction of the research. Where appropriate, identify sources of error and basic inadequacies of the technique. Do not cover up mistakes; instead, suggest ways to improve the experiment if you were to do it again. You may also speculate on the broader meaning of your conclusions in this section. Use bullets to help you present this information concisely.

7. Literature Citations

In scientific papers, it is common to cite the work of others, particularly in the Introduction and Discussion sections. The full references are then given in the References section at the end of the paper. Posters, on the other hand, are informal presentations that do not need to contain all the supporting details. Scientists who visit your poster are likely to work in the same field and probably are already familiar with most of the literature, so a long list of references would only waste valuable space on your poster. Even visitors who have a general knowledge of your topic but who work in a different subdiscipline are not interested in the details. They are interested mainly in how your approach or findings might help them improve their methodology or provide insight into their work. (Discussions with scientists in this second group are valuable to you because they provide a different perspective and may help you see applications to other subdisciplines.)

Student presentations in an in-house setting are different from poster sessions at large national meetings, because students usually do not have the background or the familiarity with the literature that career researchers have. Researching your topic is part of the scientific method, however, and presenting your work in the context of the published literature is part of good science. Thus, your instructor may ask you to include literature citations on your poster or to provide a list of references on a handout. See the section "Documenting Sources" in Chapter 4.

Poster Layout

Although the most important component of a poster is content, it is usually easier to create a poster when you have some idea of how you will visually organize the information. There is more than one way to lay out a poster.

Some posters place each data set with the corresponding method(s), result(s), and discussion in one vertical panel (see layout A below). Others place all of the methods together in one panel, place a conclusion with each figure, and summarize their collective significance in the conclusion or discussion section (see layout B below).

Create a mock layout of your poster to determine where the different elements will be placed. Since there is no specific rule as to the format of a poster (except the size, which is usually stipulated), you can design a layout that best fits your information and your audience.

Both of the following layouts are 3-column formats:

Layout A:

Title Authors and Institution		
Introduction	Figure 1 with figure legend Results or Conclusion	Discussion
Methods	Figure 2 with figure legend Results or Conclusion	Citations and Acknowledgements

Layout B:

Title Authors and Institution		
Introduction	Figure and analysis (finding)	Figure and analysis (finding)
Methods	Figure and analysis (finding)	Conclusions
Figure and analysis (finding)	Figure and analysis (finding)	Future work Citations and Acknowledgements

Poster Format

Size

Poster boards come in many sizes. Check with the conference organizer regarding minimum and maximum sizes. For poster sessions in your class, ask your instructor about appropriate materials and sizes.

Font (Type Size and Appearance)

Remember that most readers of your poster will be 3 to 6 feet away, so the print must be large and legible. Sans serif fonts like Arial are good for titles, but serif fonts like Times and Palatino are much easier to read in extended blocks of text. The **serifs** (small strokes that embellish the character at the top and bottom) create a strong horizontal emphasis, which helps the eye scan lines of text more easily.

Make the title Mixed Type or ALL CAPS in 72 point **bold**. Mixed type has the advantages of being easier to read and taking up less space than all caps. Do not use all caps if there are case-sensitive words in the title, such as pH, cDNA, or mRNA. Limit title lines to 65 characters or less.

Authors' names and affiliations should be 48 or 36 point **bold**, serif font, mixed type:

Times 48 Pt

The section headings can be 28 point **bold**, serif font, mixed type:

Times 28 Pt

The text itself should be no smaller than 24 point, serif font, mixed type, and *not* in bold:

Times 24 Pt

Poster Aesthetics

The success of a poster presentation depends on its ability to attract people from across the room. Interesting graphics and colored photos are good attention-getters, but avoid "cute" gimmicks. Present your poster in a serious and professional manner so people will take your conclusions seriously.

Organize the layout so that information flows from top left to bottom right. Align text on the left rather than centering it. The smooth left edge provides the reader with a strong visual guide through the material.

Avoid crowding. Large blocks of text turn off viewers; instead, use bullets to present your objectives and conclusions clearly and concisely. Use blank space to separate sections and to organize your poster for optimal flow from one section to the next.

Use appropriate graphics that communicate your data clearly. Use three-dimensional graphs *only* for three-dimensional data.

Colored borders around graphics and text enhance contrast, but keep framing to a minimum. **Framing** is the technique whereby the printed material is mounted on a piece of colored paper, which is mounted on a piece of different-colored paper to produce colorful borders. Use borders judiciously so that they do not distract from the poster content.

Nuts and Bolts

To affix text and figures to the poster board, use adhesive spray or glue stick. These tend to have fewer globs and bulges than liquid glues.

Ask the conference organizer (or your instructor) about how posters will be displayed at the poster session. Some possibilities include a pinch clamp on a pole, an easel, a table for self-standing posters, and cork bulletin boards to which posters are affixed with pushpins.

Presenting Your Poster

Authors should prepare a 5-minute talk explaining their poster; anticipate questions from students and instructors, and prepare appropriate answers. After this presentation, at least one author must be present at his or her poster at all times to answer questions from the session participants. The more you interact with your audience, the more feedback you are likely to receive on your work. (On the other hand, do not throw yourself on passersby who demonstrate little interest.)

Poster Checklist

- The poster layout is clear
- Title describes the outcome of the study
- Title can be visualized from at least 10 feet away
- The authors of the study and the institution are listed under the title
- The poster is divided into vertical columns
- The poster consists mostly of figures and the amount of text is kept to a minimum
- Figures and text are not crowded
- The figures can be understood without text
- The methods are provided in a flow chart format (if needed) or briefly in a figure caption
- The conclusions are highlighted
- Lengthy but significant details are provided on a handout rather than on the poster

Chapter 8

Oral Presentations

Scientific findings are communicated through journal articles, poster presentations at meetings, and oral presentations. Oral presentations are different from journal articles and posters because the speaker's delivery plays a critical role in the success of the communication.

The most natural form of oral presentation is extemporaneous, whereby the speaker has carefully prepared the presentation beforehand, rehearsed it, and may use an outline to stay on track during the actual talk. Most of your lectures in biology classes are likely to be extemporaneous presentations, so you may already have some experience with the characteristics that make this type of oral presentation successful:

- The speaker establishes a good rapport with the audience.

- The presentation is well organized and leaves listeners satisfied that they understand more than they did before.

- The visuals are simple, legible, and help listeners focus on the important points.

Organization

Extemporaneous presentations are not unlike scientific papers in their structure, but they are much more selective in their content. As in a scientific paper, the **introduction** captures the audience's attention, provides background information on the subject, and clarifies the objectives of the work (Table 8.1). The **body** is a condensed version of the Materials and Methods and Results sections, and contains only the details necessary to emphasize and support the speaker's conclusions. If the focus of the talk is on the results, then the speaker spends less time on the methods and more time on visuals that highlight the findings. The visuals may be simpler than those prepared for a journal article, because the audience may

TABLE 8.1 Comparison of the structure of an oral presentation
and a journal article

ORAL PRESENTATION	JOURNAL ARTICLE
	Abstract
Introduction	Introduction
Body	Materials and Methods, Results
Closing	Discussion
	References

only have a minute or two to digest the material in the visual (in contrast
to a journal article, where the reader can re-read the paper as often as
desired). Finally, the **closing** is comparable to the Discussion section,
because here the speaker summarizes the objectives and results, states
conclusions, and emphasizes the take-home message for the audience.

There is no distinct Abstract or References section in an oral presentation. If the presentation is part of a meeting, an Abstract may be provided in the program. If listeners are interested in the references, they should
contact the speaker after the talk.

Plan Ahead

Before you start writing the content of your presentation, make sure you
know

- Your audience. What do they know? What do they want to know?
- Why you are giving the talk, not just why you did the experiment. Are you informing the audience, or are you trying to persuade them to adopt your point of view?
- Your speaking environment. How much time do you have?
  How large is the audience? What audio-visual equipment is
  available (chalkboard, overhead projector, computer with projection equipment)?

Write the Text

An oral presentation will actually take you longer to prepare than a
paper. D'Arcy (1998) breaks down the steps as follows:

- Procrastination   25%

- Research   30%
- Writing and creating visuals   40%
- Rehearsal   5%

To overcome procrastination, follow the same strategy as for writing a laboratory report: write the body first (Materials and Methods and Results sections), then the introduction, and finally the closing.

- Write the main points of each section in outline form.
- Use the primary literature (journal articles) to provide background in the introduction and supporting references in the closing.
- Transfer your outline to notecards. Use only one side of the notecards, and limit yourself to one main topic per card. Note where you plan to use visual aids.
- If you plan to use a presentation graphics program such as Microsoft PowerPoint in addition to notecards, make sure each slide is just an *outline* of what you're going to say. Use the slides to *support* what you say, not *repeat* what you say.
- Keep it short and simple. Tell your audience what you're *going* to tell them, *tell* them, and then tell them what you *told* them.

Prepare the Visuals

Effective visual aids help the audience to visualize the data and to see relationships among variables. They clarify information that would otherwise involve lengthy descriptions.

Effective visuals are simple, legible, and organized logically. They capture the listener's interest, increase comprehension, and focus attention on the important findings. When deciding on which visuals to use, keep in mind that student audiences prefer figures to tables. For guidelines on what kind of figure to use, see "Visuals" and "Organizing Your Data" in Chapter 4. For instructions on how to make XY graphs in Microsoft Excel, see Appendix 2. Photos, diagrams, and drawings are effective ways to show physical rather than numerical results. Mechanisms are much easier to visualize when the verbal description is accompanied by a drawing.

Take the time to make good visuals for your oral presentation. We receive more than 83% of our information through sight, and only 11% through hearing. Without visuals, your listeners will forget most of your presentation within 8 hours. These statistics help explain why Microsoft PowerPoint has become so popular in recent years. PowerPoint allows you to create a slide show containing text, graphics, and even animations

(A)

(B)

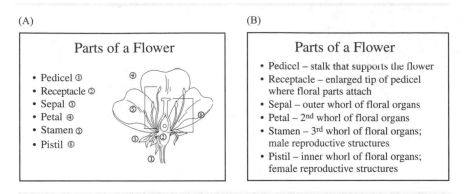

Figure 8.1 Effective (A) and less effective (B) ways to use text on a slide. The wording in Slide A is simple and the numbered reference to the figure makes it easy for viewers to visualize the location of each floral part. The large amount of text on Slide B will have the audience reading instead of listening to the speaker, and the absence of a diagram slows comprehension.

(see Appendix 3). PowerPoint has the same advantages as word processing programs in that it is easy to make revisions and even send an electronic copy of the presentation to a colleague to review.

Because PowerPoint is so easy to use, you may be tempted to write every word of your presentation on the slides. Don't do it. Follow these tips for preparing visuals:

- **Do not put too much information on any one slide or transparency.** A good rule of thumb is to cover only one concept per slide or transparency; use overlays for more complicated concepts that require more than one slide.

- **Keep the wording simple.** Instead of using full sentences, bullet keywords or key points (Figure 8.1). Limit the number of key points to 3–6.

- **Make sure the lettering can be read from anywhere in the room.** Use no smaller than 18–24 pt sans serif font and black type on a white background for best contrast. The light background makes the room much brighter, which has the dual advantage of keeping the audience awake and allowing you to see your listener's faces. Use color sparingly in text slides; a bright color or a larger font, when used sparingly, are good ways to emphasize a point.

- **Use the same font and format for each slide for a consistent look.** Avoid "cute" graphics that might detract from the scientific message.
- **Keep graphs simple.** Make the numbers and the lettering on the axis labels large and legible. Choose symbols that are easy to distinguish. Instead of following the conventions used in journal articles, modify the figure format as follows (Figure 8.2):

(A)

Figure 1 Beta-galactosidase production in *E. coli* grown under three different conditions. The mutant strain, which produces a nonfunctional repressor protein, was grown in glycerol. The wild-type strain was grown in glycerol, with or without the addition of IPTG (a lactose analog) at $t = 0$ min.

(B)

Figure 8.2   Example of figure formatting for (A) a journal article and (B) an oral presentation

- Position the title *above* the figure and *don't* number it. The title should reflect your most important finding.

- Label each line instead of identifying the data symbols with a key. The labels may be made using textboxes in Excel, Word, or PowerPoint.

Both of these modifications make it easier for the listener to digest the information within the short time the graph is displayed during the presentation.

- **Use symbols consistently in all of your graphs.** For example, if you use a triangle to represent "Mutant in glycerol" in the first graph, use the same symbol for the same condition in the rest of your graphs.

- **Appeal to your listeners' multiple senses.** Use images from the Internet, recordings of heart sounds or bird songs, and animations or movie clips if they help make your point. Make sure these "extras" do not detract from your take-home message and that they fit within the time limit of your presentation.

- **Allow at least 20 seconds for each slide, more time for complicated slides.**

Rehearsal

After you have written your presentation and prepared your visuals, you must practice your delivery. Give yourself plenty of time so that you can run through your presentation several times and, if possible, do a practice presentation in the same room where you will hold the actual presentation. Here are some other tips:

- Go to a place where you can be alone and undisturbed. Read your presentation aloud, paying attention to the organization. Does one topic flow into the next, or are their awkward transitions? Revise as needed.

- Time yourself. Make sure your presentation does not exceed the time limit.

- After you are satisfied with the organization, flow, and length, ask a friend to listen to your presentation. Ask him or her to evaluate your poise, posture, voice (clarity, volume, and rate), gestures and mannerisms, and interaction with the audience (eye contact, ability to recognize if the audience is following your talk).

It is natural to be nervous when you begin speaking to an audience, even an audience of your classmates. Adequate knowledge of the subject, good preparation, and sufficient rehearsal can all help to reduce your nervousness and enhance your self-assurance.

Delivery

The importance of the delivery cannot be overstated: listeners pay more attention to body language (50%) and voice (30%) than to the content (20%) (Fegert and others 2002). Remember that you must establish a good rapport with the audience in order for your oral presentation to be successful. The following guidelines will help.

Presentation Style

- Number your notecards so that if you drop them you can reassemble them quickly.

- Dress appropriately for the occasion.

- Use good posture. Good posture is equated with self-assurance, while slouching implies a lack of confidence.

- Be positive and enthusiastic about your subject.

- Try to maintain eye contact with some members of the audience. Eye contact is perceived as more personal, as though the speaker is talking with individual listeners.

- Avoid distracting gestures and mannerisms such as pacing, fidgeting with the pointer, jingling the change in your pocket, and adjusting your hair and clothes.

- Speak clearly, at a rate that is neither too fast nor too slow, and make sure your voice carries to the back of the room. Avoid "um's," "ah's," and other nervous sounds.

Integrating Visuals

Visuals are an integral part of an oral presentation. If you are writing on a chalkboard or dry erase board, be sure to:

- Write neatly

- Not stand in front of what you have written

- Use large print

- Select a color that can be easily seen from the back of the class-room

If you use **PowerPoint** to prepare your presentation:

- Do not stand behind the computer monitor and read your presentation off the screen. This practice distances you from your audience.

No matter which method you choose, the following points apply:

- Do not display a visual until you are ready to discuss it.

- Stand next to the projection screen and point with your outstretched arm or pointer (stick) or use a laser pointer.

- Tell the audience exactly what to look for. Interpret statistics and numbers so that they are meaningful to your listeners. If you are describing Figure 8.2, for example, "Beta-galactosidase production increased dramatically in only 10 minutes after adding the lactose analog" is likely to make a bigger impression on the audience than "The absorbance increased from 0.12 to 0.71 in only 10 minutes after adding the lactose analog."

- Point to the specific part of the visual that illustrates what you are describing. Avoid waving the pointer in the general direction of the visual.

- Do not block the projected image with your body.

- Do not turn your back on the audience.

Interacting with the Audience

A unique benefit of communicating information verbally is that you can adjust your presentation based on the feedback you receive from your listeners. Pay attention to the reaction of individuals in the audience. Does their posture or facial expression suggest interest, boredom, or confusion? If you perceive that the audience is not following you, ask a question or two, and adjust your delivery according to their response. Your willingness to customize your presentation to your audience will enhance your reputation and lead to greater listener satisfaction.

To keep listeners focused:

- Establish common ground immediately. Ask a question or describe a general phenomenon with which your audience is familiar.

- Make sure your introduction is well organized and proceeds logically from the general to the specific without any sidetracks.

- Alert your audience when you plan to change topics. Practice these transitions when you rehearse.

- Summarize the main points from time to time. Tell your listeners what you want them to remember.

- Use examples to illustrate your hypotheses and conclusions.

- End your presentation with a definite statement such as "In conclusion…" Don't fade out weakly with phrases such as "Well, that's about it."

Group Presentations

If you are presenting with another person, your individual contributions should complement one another, not compete with each other. This requires good coordination and practice beforehand.

Fielding Listener Questions

Allow time for questions and discussion. Take questions as a compliment—your listeners were paying attention! Listen carefully to each question, repeat it so that everyone in the room can hear, and then give a brief, thoughtful response. If you don't understand the question, ask the listener to rephrase it. If you don't know the answer, say so.

Signal the end of the question session with "We have time for one more question" or something similar.

Feedback

It takes not only practice, but also coaching, to become an effective speaker. When you make an oral presentation to your class, your instructor may ask your classmates to evaluate your delivery, organization, and visual aids, as well as the thoroughness of your research using a form such as the "Evaluation Form for Oral Presentations" available at <http: www.sinauer.com/Knisely>.

When you are in the position of the listener, make the kinds of comments you would find helpful if you were the speaker. As you know, feedback is most likely to be appreciated when it is constructive, specific, and done in an atmosphere of mutual respect.

WORD PROCESSING BASICS IN MICROSOFT WORD 2007

If you have been writing papers in Microsoft Word for a while and have recently updated to Office 2007, you've probably been frustrated by the changes to once familiar commands and menus. Fear not, in this appendix we will try to help you find your way in this strange new program. Sections 1–3 deal with very basic functions that have not changed much. You may find Section 3.6, "Tracking Changes Made by Peer Reviewers," helpful during the revision process. If you want to save time inserting Greek letters and mathematical symbols, italics, and subscripts and superscripts, or if you want to replace long chemical names with a shorter keystroke combination, look over Section 4, which covers special functions in scientific papers.

The screen drops in this appendix are for Microsoft Word 2007 on a PC. Path notation for reaching a particular command or option is shown relative to a command on the menu bar, toolbar, or task bar. For example, **Office Button | New | Blank Document** means "Click the Office Button, then click New, then select Blank Document." These general instructions apply to Word 2008 on Macintosh computers as well, although there are some differences, such as the use of the Option key in place of the Control key.

1. Good Housekeeping Habits

1.1 File Organization

You can expect to type at least one major paper and perhaps several minor writing assignments in every college course each semester. This amounts to a fair number of documents on your hard disk and removable disks (CDs, flash drives, etc.). Good file organization is important for several reasons:

- When you are writing papers in different subjects at different times during the semester, you need to have a simple, logical system that will allow you to find the files you are working on.

Nothing is more frustrating than to have a deadline and waste precious time searching for the wanted file.

- If your instructor informs you that he/she never received your paper, you will be expected to print out another copy. Excuses such as "I can't find the file" or "I accidentally erased it" are not viewed favorably.

- If you are asked to be a teaching assistant for an introductory course, it is helpful to be able to refer to your old lab reports when students ask you questions. The compactness and convenience of an electronic copy can't be beat.

When setting up a filing system on your computer, think of the computer as a large filing cabinet, with the drawers representing the computer's drives. Typically the hard drive is the **C:** drive, the floppy drive is **A:**, and, if present, the CD (compact disk) and flash drives are given other letter designations.

In a paper filing cabinet, the drawers contain folders, the folders may be further subdivided into subfolders, and the subfolders contain the actual documents. Word creates a "My Documents" folder on the hard drive as a possible location for storing your files. You can create subfolders within "My Documents," or you can create folders in addition to "My Documents."

One way to organize your files is by course number. Within each course, you could create subfolders for different assignments, such as lecture notes, homework, or lab reports. If you expect to have only a few assignments that require work on the computer, you may not even need to make subfolders.

There are two easy ways to create folders or subfolders. One way is to use Windows Explorer, and the other way is to make folders within Word.

Creating folders in Word. When you open Word, a blank document appears. At the top of the screen, there is the Office Button with the Quick Access Toolbar and what Microsoft calls "The Ribbon," which contains a number of tabs related to different sets of tools (Figure A1.1). To open a previously created document, click **Office Button | Open** and locate the file or choose a recently used file from the list.

To create a new folder in Word:

1. Click **Office Button | Save As**. The **Save As** dialog box appears.

2. Click the down arrow next to the **Save in** text box to locate the folder in which you want to create a subfolder.

3. Click the **Create New Folder** button. The keyboard shortcut for this is **Alt+ F4**. The **New Folder** dialog box appears (Figure A1.2).

4. Type a name for the new folder and click **OK**.

The new folder now appears in the **Save As** dialog box.

Figure A1.1 Screen display of a blank Word 2007 document with the Quick Access Toolbar and Ribbon.

1.2 Saving your Files

One of the most important tasks you must learn when working on the computer is saving your files. When you write the first draft of a paper by hand, you have tangible evidence that you have done the work. When you type something on the computer, however, your work is unprotected until you

Figure A1.2 Save As dialog box allows you to create folders and subfolders in Word.

save it. That means that if the power goes off or the computer crashes before you save the file, you have to start again from scratch. Hopefully it won't take the loss of a night's work to convince you to make sure you know how to save your files!

Save your work often. The more difficult or complicated the text, the more often you should save it. Think about how long you would need to retype the text if it were lost and whether you can afford to spend that much time redoing it.

Naming and saving files manually.   Although AutoSave (described in the next section) provides some insurance against lost work, saving your file manually produces a permanent file that will still be there if the power goes off or the computer crashes.

Do not wait until you are finished typing the document to save a file—save it after you have written the first sentence. Even though Word and other word processors save files in a temporary memory, your work is not protected unless it has been saved in a permanent form.

1. **To save your file for the first time,** click **Office Button | Save As** (see Figure A1.1). The **Save As** dialog box appears (see Figure A1.2).

2. You have to make three important decisions when saving a file for the first time:
   - Location (drive, folder, and subfolder, if applicable)
   - File name
   - File extension (format)

The default **location** where the current document will be saved is shown in the **Save in** text box. To change to another folder or another drive, click the arrow next to the text box. Double-click the drive, folder, or subfolder until you arrive at the location where you want to save the current document. Only the folders for the selected drive will be displayed. To see the folders in another drive, double-click the desired drive.

You will need to choose a **file name**. The name suggested by Word is shown in the **File name** text box near the bottom of the dialog box. You may wish to replace Word's suggestion with a descriptive name that allows you to find it easily when you do future revisions. Sometimes you may also want to keep track of different versions of the same document by appending the file name with a number or letter (e.g., Protein1.docx, Protein2.docx, etc.).

Windows machines automatically assign a **file extension** (the three or four letters following the period in the file name) based on the program you are working in. It is best not to change the extension unless you expect to open the file in a different program. Some common file extensions are shown below. When you have entered the location, file name, and file extension, click **Save** to save the file and close the dialog box.

Program Extension

Word	.doc (2003 & earlier), .docx (2007)
Excel	.xls (2003 & earlier), .xlsx (2007)
PowerPoint	.ppt (2003 & earlier), .pptx (2007)
Adobe Acrobat	.pdf
Images	.jpg, .tif, .gif
HTML	.html, .htm, .htx

To save the same file subsequently, click the **Save** button (it's in the Quick Access Toolbar), or **File | Save** in the menu of the Office Button. You can also save files using the keyboard by pressing Ctrl+S.

To save the same file at a different location, under a different name, or with a different file extension:

1. Click **Office Button | Save As** on the menu bar (or press the F12 key). The **Save As** dialog box appears (see Figure A1.2).

2. Change the location, name, or extension as needed.

3. Click **Save** to save the file and close the dialog box.

Often, your instructor will ask you to e-mail a file to him or her. One way to insure that your instructor is able to read it is to save it as a PDF. Most computers (PCs and Macs) have no trouble opening up a .pdf file. Word 2007 has a built-in function to create these files. Go to **Office Button | Save As | PDF** (or **Adobe PDF** if you have it). This will open the Save As dialog box; enter a name and press **Save**. Be sure to always check with your instructor for the proper file format to use.

AutoSave. AutoSave automatically saves the file you are currently working in at specified intervals. It should be considered a backup to (not a substitute for) saving the file manually.

1. To activate AutoSave, click **Office Button | Word Options** on the bottom of the menu.

2. Select the **Save** tab in the **Options** dialog box (Figure A1.3). Select:
   - Save AutoRecover info every: ___ Minutes (use the arrow to specify the interval, e.g., 10 minutes)
   - Save Word files as: Word Document (.docx)

AutoSave saves the document in a **recovery file**. This feature is not a substitute for manually saving documents, because the recovery file is deleted

Figure A1.3 Options dialog box, Save tab.

when you save or close a document. If the power goes off, the recovery file still exists. When you restart Word, Word opens the recovery file so that you can save it manually. If you do not save the recovery file, it is deleted.

Backup files. It is very, very important to make at least one backup copy of your file while you are writing an important paper. The backup file should be saved on a removable disk, not on your hard drive. If your hard drive goes down, having a backup copy on a removable disk means you have not lost your work; you can continue working on your paper on another computer.

To make a backup file, follow the first set of instructions in Section 1.2. Change the location to one of your computer's removable disk drives or use a USB Flash Drive (also called JumpDrive or Thumb drive) to transfer files from one computer to another. Depending on capacity, flash drives hold as much as or more than a CD, yet they are only the size of a stick of gum.

1.3 Protecting Your Files Against Viruses and Worms

Keep your antivirus software up to date by downloading the most recent software from the company's Internet site. New viruses and worms infect someone's computer every day, so you must aggressively protect your system and all the time invested in writing your papers. An ounce of prevention is worth a pound of cure, as the saying goes.

1.4 Removing Files

If you use your computer a lot, and especially if you have large files and graphics, the disk space fills up fast. Your computer will give you a message when you are running out of disk space. That is a sign that you need to remove files from the hard drive(s).

   If you have already backed up an inactive file (one on which you are no longer working) on a removable disk, then you can delete this file from the hard drive. Also check for files in the Recycling Bin, as well as for temporary files, files attached to e-mail messages, and images saved from the Internet. Copying these files to removable disks and then deleting them from the hard disk frees up valuable space on your computer.

Deleting files using Word. You can easily delete individual files in Word using these steps:

1. Click **Office Button | Open**.
2. Locate the file you want to delete (you may have to change drives or folders).
3. Right-click the unwanted file, and select **Delete**, or just press the **Delete** key.

2. Formatting a Document

All scientific journals have a section devoted to instructions for authors. These instructions tell the author exactly how to format a paper, so that all the papers in the journal have a uniform appearance. If your instructor has not given you specific instructions, the layout in Table A1.1 will lend a professional look to your lab report or scientific paper. If you are already familiar with Word, the Quick Reference tells you where to make these formatting adjustments. Detailed instructions are given in the sections following the table.

TABLE A1.1 Giving your document a professional appearance

FEATURE	LAYOUT	QUICK REFERENCE
Paper	8½ x 11" (or DIN A4) white bond, print double sided if you can	Page Layout Tab | Page setup | Corner Icon | Paper
Margins	1" left and right;1" top and bottom	Page Layout Tab | Page setup | Margins
Font size	12 pt (points to the inch)	Home Tab | Font
Typeface	Times Roman (serif) or Helvetica (sans serif). Serif fonts are easier to read for most people, but sans serif fonts are favored in graphics and presentations.	Home Tab | Font
Pagination	Arabic number, top right on each page except the first	Insert Tab | Header and Footer | Page Number
Page Break	To maintain section continuity	Ctrl + Enter or Insert Tab | Pages | Page Break
Spacing	Double	Home Tab | Paragraph | Spacing Icon
New paragraph	Indent 0.5"	This is usually the default setting. To change it go to Home Tab | Paragraph | Corner Icon
Aligning text	**Justification** is Left/ragged right or Justify/even edges **Indent** entire paragraph to set off from rest of text **Tabs** **Lists** that begin with Bullets or Numbers	All of these commands are found in Home Tab | Paragraph

2.1 Toolbars and The Ribbon

When you open Word, a blank document appears. At the top of the screen, there is the office button next to the Quick Access Toolbar, and then the Ribbon with various tabs for different sets of tools. If you are accustomed to having the menu bar available, you will find the Ribbon a nuisance.

You still can personalize your tools to some extent, but not as much as in Office 2003. To personalize your Quick Access Toolbar, right click on it and then select **Customize Quick Access Toolbar**, and clear or select the check boxes according to your preferences. Unfortunately, you cannot customize the Ribbon.

TABLE A1.1 Continued

FEATURE	LAYOUT	QUICK REFERENCE
Title page (optional)	Title, authors (your name first, lab partner second), class, and date	
Headings	Align headings for Abstract, Introduction, Materials and Methods, Results, Discussion, and References on left margin or center them. Use consistent format for capitalization.	Home Tab | Styles | Heading 1.
Subheadings	Use sparingly and maintain consistent format	Home Tab | Styles | Heading 2, Heading 3, etc.
References	Name-Year System: Use hanging indent to list references. Use accepted punctuation and format.	Home Tab| Paragraph | Corner Icon | Special | Hanging by 0.25"
Tables and Figures	Important tables and figures are often embedded in the text or placed in an appendix. Tables can be made in Excel and copied and pasted in or can be made directly in Word. Figures are either pasted in or inserted through Word.	Insert Tab | Table | then select number of cells This will open a separate Table Tools Tab with table formatting options. Insert Tab | Picture | select picture file. This will also open a separate Picture Tools Tab.
Assembly	Pages in order, staple top left corner	

The **Ribbon** consists of pictorial buttons that are grouped together in tabs. If you place the mouse pointer over a particular button (do not click any mouse buttons), a description of that button will appear.

The tabs that are important for formatting your document are **Home, Insert**, and **Page Layout**. Often, there will be an arrow in the lower right corner of a tab that you can click to open more familiar dialog boxes for changing settings.

2.2 Paper

Click **Page Layout Tab | Page Setup | Corner Icon** on the Ribbon. You will find three tabs: Margins, Paper, and Layout (Figure A1.4). Choose the orientation of the paper (portrait vs. landscape) on the **Margins** tab. To change paper size, click the **Paper** tab, then click the arrow button and make your selection.

Figure A1.4 Page Setup
Corner Icon dialog box.

2.3 Margins

Click **Page Layout Tab | Page Setup | Margins** on the Ribbon. You could also go through the Corner Icon dialog box as in the above section (see Figure A1.4). Select the Margin option you want from the Margins button. Normal is 1″ margins all the way around. You can customize the margins if you need to. The Gutter refers to the amount of space between multiple columns on a page.

2.4 Font Size and Typeface

Serif fonts such as Times Roman are easier to read for most people than sans serif fonts such as Arial. The most legible point size generally seems to be 12. Thus, for most machines, the default Normal font is 12 pt Times New Roman. Presentations are generally easier to read from a distance when they are in sans serif fonts.

To modify the font style, size, or appearance, click **Home Tab | Font** on the Ribbon. To apply formatting to existing text, you must first select the text that you want to format. To select a word, double-click it. To select a paragraph, triple-click anywhere within the paragraph. To select a block of text, use one of the methods described in Section 2.7.

2.5 Page Numbers

Click **Insert Tab | Header and Footer | Page Number** on the Ribbon. When you click **on Page Number**, you can select the position (top or bottom of the page) and the alignment (left, center, right, inside, or outside) of the page numbers from a pop-up menu. Journal articles tend to have the page numbers placed at the bottom, on the outside margins. For your course work, however, bottom right is fine. You will probably not want to have a page number on the first page of your lab report. You can prevent this from happening by clicking **Format Page Numbers** from the pop-up menu. In the **Start At field**, type in **2**. All pages of your paper except the first page should have a page number, so that you can easily determine the order of the pages and whether all pages are present.

By convention, Arabic numerals are used to number the pages. This style is the default page number format in Word. In some special situations (e.g., Table of Contents or Preface of a book), Roman numerals or letters are used. These alternative formats can be selected by clicking the **Format Page Numbers** button.

Figure A1.5 Page Numbers dialog box.

The font of the page number should be the same as the font of your text. Because page numbers are part of the header or footer, you can check the page number font by displaying the header and footer. Simply click on the Header or Footer area of your page and you can format the text.

Double-click the page number to open up a special tab on the Ribbon called **Header and Footer Tools | Design**.

2.6 Page Breaks

A **page break** will insert a new page at the position of the cursor. If it precedes text, then that text will appear on the new page. For example, let's say that you start a new section of your lab report or scientific paper near the bottom of a page. Perhaps the section heading fits, but the rest of the text gets thrown onto the next page. To make sure that the section heading is not separated from the rest of the text, position the cursor just in front of the heading. Click **Insert Tab | Pages | Page Break**. A faster way to do this is to put the cursor just in front of the heading and press Ctrl + Enter on the keyboard.

2.7 Line Spacing

Line spacing refers to the amount of space between lines on a page and is found under **Home Tab | Paragraph | Line Spacing Icon** on the Ribbon. The default setting is now 1.15; in Word 2003 it was Single. To change line spacing before you begin typing your paper, select **Double** under **Line Spacing in the Paragraph** Corner Icon dialog box (Figure A1.6) or click the **Line Spacing** Icon and select "**2**." To adjust line spacing at a later time, **select the block of text** to be changed by either of the following methods:

- Hold down the left mouse button, and drag the cursor across the text from the first character to the last.
- Click the left mouse button at the beginning of the text, hold down the Shift key, and click the last word in the block. This method works well when the text extends over several paragraphs or even pages.

When the block of text is selected, follow the aforementioned procedure to adjust line spacing.

A new feature in Word 2007 is to have the default Style to be "Normal." Now, you may find this confusing because you may think Normal would refer to a document that doesn't have any format changes yet. However, in Word 2007 Normal refers to the style in which there is an extra space between each paragraph (every time you press enter). To change this, go to **Home Tab | Styles** and choose the style you want for your document. It is recommended that if you want to change the style, you should do it right

Figure A1.6 Paragraph dialog
box, Indents and Spacing tab.

Figure A1.6 Paragraph dialog box, Indents and Spacing tab.

at the beginning of your document before you start typing. If you choose to do it later, Word will continually return to the default Normal style. For more information, see Section 2.14.

2.8 Aligning Text

There are a number of different ways to align text in a Word document. The ones you are most likely to use are as follows:

- Justification (right, left, center, or full). **See Section 2.9**.
- Indenting an entire paragraph so that it is set off from the rest of the text. **See Section 2.10**.
- Tabs. **See Section 2.11**.
- Lists that begin with numbers or bullets. **See Section 2.13**.

Never use the space bar to align text, because variation in character size will lead to variation in vertical text alignment as well.

2.9 Justification

Justification is the adjustment of the lines so that they are aligned either on the left margin (with ragged right edge), centered between the margins, aligned on the right margin (with ragged left edge), or aligned both on the left and right margin (with even edges). Under **Home Tab | Paragraph**, you will find four icons for your justification options.

2.10 Indentation

Indenting a block of text allows you to change the margins, so that only that block of text will be set off from the others.

To indent text, click **Home Tab | Paragraph | Corner Icon** on the Ribbon. On the **Indents and Spacing** tab in the dialog box that opens (see Figure A1.6), set the left and right Indentation as desired (for example, 1″). When you type the text, it will be set off from the rest of the text with wider margins. Pressing **Enter** and then **Backspace** returns the indentation to the default values.

If you have already typed a passage that you later decide you want to indent:

1. Select the passage by one of the methods described in Section 2.7.

2. Click **Home Tab | Paragraph | Corner Icon**.

3. Set the desired indentation on the **Indents and Spacing** tab.

4. Click **OK**.

2.11 Tabs

Tab stops allow you to jump a set distance forward on a line. It is always preferable to use tab stops rather than the space bar to align text in columns. Because character spacing varies with the size of the characters in a font, different words, even though they have the same number of characters, occupy different-sized spaces on a line. Adding more spaces will not change this mismatch. Instead, put the words on a tab stop, which defines the vertical alignment regardless of the characters. Remember, **never use the space bar to align text in columns!** (For multiple columns, also see **Section 2.12,** "Tables with no lines.")

To adjust tab stops, select **Home Tab | Paragraph | Corner Icon | Tabs** (it's on the bottom of the dialog window). The default tab stops are given in the top right corner of the **Tabs** dialog box and will most likely be 0.5″. Change the default if desired, or add individual tab stops as needed.

The indentation that designates a new paragraph is determined by the first tab stop in the default setting. The customary paragraph indentation is 0.5″.

2.12 Creating a Table

By convention, tables in scientific papers do not have vertical lines to separate the columns, and horizontal lines are used only to separate the table caption from the column headings, the headings from the data, and the data from any footnotes (see, for example, Table 1 in Figure 4.2).

To create a table:

1. Position the cursor where you want to insert the table.

2. Click on the **Insert Tab** | **Tables** on the Ribbon. Mouse over the number of columns and rows.

A blank table appears with the cursor in the first cell.

Tables with no lines. To align text in columns without showing any lines:

1. After you create a table as described above, two new tab options open up on the Ribbon: **Table Tools** | **Design** and **Table Tools** | **Layout**. Click **Table Tools** | **Layout** | **Table** | **Properties**, then click the **Borders and Shading** button in the dialog box that opens.

2. On the **Borders** tab, select **None**.

3. Click **OK**.

Navigation in tables. To **jump** from one cell to an adjacent one, use the arrow keys. To move forward across the row, use the **Tab** key. *Note:* If you press **Tab** when you are in the last cell of the table, Word adds another row to the table.

To align text on a tab stop in a table cell, press Ctrl+Tab.

Inserting and deleting rows or columns. To insert a new column or row, position the cursor in a cell adjacent to where you want to insert a new column or row. Select **Table Tools** | **Layout Tab** | **Rows and Columns** and then the desired location (Columns to the left, Columns to the right, Rows above, or Rows below).

To delete a column, row, or individual cell, position the cursor in the column, row, or cell you want to delete. Select **Table Tools** | **Layout Tab** | **Delete** and make your selection or you can also highlight the row or column and right click on it to find a delete command.

Changing column width or row height. To change the width of a column, position the cursor on one of the vertical lines so that [insert column width icon here] appears. Then hold down the left mouse button and move the line to make the column the desired width. To change the height of a row, position the cursor on one of the horizontal lines so that [insert column width icon here] appears. Then hold down the left mouse button and move the line to make the row the desired height.

Other table commands. Position the cursor in the table, and then click **Table Tools** on the Ribbon. Other commands for customizing your table are shown in the two tabs for Table Tools.

You can format the text in each cell just as you would format running text. For example, to center the column headings or to put them in boldface, select the top row and click the **Center** or **Bold** button on the Home Tab.

To align numbers, select the entire column and click the **Align Right** button. To format all the cells, click the top left cell, hold down the **Shift** key, and click the bottom right cell. To format selected cells, do the same, except hold down the **Ctrl** key.

2.13 Lists That Begin with Numbers or Bullets

A **numbered list** is often used to organize your thoughts first as an outline. A **bulleted list** is handy for highlighting or summarizing the main points of a paper or poster, when chronological order is not important.

To make a bulleted list:

1. Click **Home Tab | Bullets Icon** on the Ribbon.

2. Choose the pull down menu from the **Bullet Icon** to make an unnumbered list. You have a choice of eight bullets: none and symbols such as filled dots, open dots, arrows, and boxes. Click the one you want.

3. If you prefer a different bullet, press the **Define New Bullet** button at the bottom of the pull down menu. In the **Define New Bullet** dialog box (Figure A1.7), click the **Symbol** button. This opens the **Symbols** dialog box, which allows you to change the font to any ASCII character.

4. Also in the **Define New Bullet** dialog box, you can make a picture of your choice a bullet. Some are already suggested there, but you can also import an image file and have your bullets be tiny pictures. This is not recommended for your lab reports, but it's fun to play with.

5. Again in the **Customize Bulleted List** dialog box, click the **Font** button. This allows you to change the size or style of the bullet.

6. Finally, set the indentation of the bullet and the text. If you want the bullet to start on the left margin, set the indentation to 0". Set the text indentation 0.25" more than the bullet indentation. Click **OK**.

Figure A1.7 Customize Bulleted list dialog box.

7. Every time you press **Enter** at the end of a statement, a new bullet appears on the next line.

8. When you have finished typing the list, press **Enter**, and then **Backspace** to delete the new bullet.

You can also type a list first, and then add bullets later on. To do this, select the passage by one of the methods described in Section 2.7, and then select **Home Tab | Bullets or Numbering Icon**, and the desired format.

To make a numbered list, follow a similar procedure as with a bulleted list:

1. Click **Home Tab | Numbering Icon** on the Ribbon.

2. You have a choice of eight options: none and different styles of numbers or letters. Click the one you want.

3. If you prefer another option, click the **Define New Number Format** at the bottom of the pull down menu. In the **Define New Number Format** dialog box, set the Number format, style, and position.

4. You can also select how you want the list numbered: **Restart numbering**, or **Continue previous list**. Find these options in the **Home Tab | Numbering Icon** pull-down menu. Click **Set Numbering Value**. If you didn't have any previous numbered list of that format, these selections will not be available.

Even though it is practical to number the steps in a procedure for your own reference, this is **never** done in scientific papers. The procedures are always written in paragraph form in the Materials and Methods section, never as a numbered list.

2.14 Style

A **style** is a set of formats that can be applied to a few words, a paragraph, or a whole document. Look on the right side of the **Home Tab** for the Styles group. You can scroll through your options there or click the corner icon to open up a dialog box.

Scientific papers and laboratory reports are divided into sections, and each section begins with a heading (for example, **Introduction**). To ensure that your section headings are uniform, click the down arrow next to the Style box and select Heading 1. Formatting is automatically applied as you type the heading. Press **Enter** and the formatting of the subsequent text returns to normal. For subheadings, select Heading 2, Heading 3, and so on (Figure A1.8).

Headings are also used to generate a table of contents, so you might find this feature useful for longer research papers.

To change the characteristics of a style:

1. Click the **Styles corner icon** to open the dialog box.

2. In the dialog box, right-click the style you want to modify.

3. Click **Modify** to open the **Modify Style** dialog box and change the characteristics as needed.

4. Click **OK**.

Figure A1.8 Style dialog box.

2.15 Templates

Templates specify the format of all Word documents. When you select **File | New** from the Office Button, Word prompts you to choose a new document template. Blank Document is the default template. If your instructor has specified a particular format for all your papers, you can customize an existing template for the format you need.

Follow these steps:

Figure A1.9 Templates available in Word. In Word 2007, this window is opened when you begin a new file.

1. Select **File | New** from the Office Button.

2. Click on My Templates… on the left side of the dialog box (Figure A1.9).

3. Click the Template Button in the Create New section of the dialog box that opens.

4. Check the settings for each feature in Table A1.1, or your instructor's specifications, and make changes where necessary.

5. Select **File | Save As** from the Office Button. The **Save As** type will automatically be **Document Template (*.dot)**.

6. Type the name of the new template next to File name. For example, you might give the template the same name as your course.

Every time you type papers for that course, select **File | New**, and then click the course icon. Using the same template gives your documents a uniform appearance. If your template does not appear in the **Recently Used Templates**, then click **My Templates** and click the **Document Button** in the **Create New** section. Once you have used your new template more than once then it will appear in the **Recently Used Templates** menu.

3. Editing the Text

You will modify parts of your document while you are writing it, as well as afterwards during the editing and proofreading stages. Some of the most common modifications involve:

TABLE A1.2 Quick reference for editing command

FEATURE	QUICK REFERENCE
Views	View Tab | Document Views, Show/Hide, Zoom, Window
Zoom	View Tab | Zoom
Cut, Copy, and Paste	Home Tab | Clipboard
	Keyboard Shortcuts: Ctrl + X (cut), Ctrl + C (copy), Ctrl + V (paste)
Find, Replace	Home Tab | Editing | Find or Replace
	Keyboard Shortcuts: Ctrl + F (find), Ctrl + H (replace)
Spelling and grammar checker	Review Tab | Proofing | Spelling and Grammar
Manual, systematic spelling and grammar checker	Highlight the text in question, then click Spelling and Grammar, as above, or right click on the underlined text.
Word count	Review Tab | Proofing | Word Count
	Word also keeps a running count of your words in the bottom left corner of the Word window.
Tracking changes made by peer reviewers	Review Tab | Tracking | Track changes
	You can also modify what you track by clicking on the pull down menu from Track Changes.

- Views
- Cut, copy, and paste
- Find and replace
- Spelling and grammar checker
- Word count
- Tracking changes made by peer reviewers

Use Table A1.2 if you are already familiar with these features. Detailed instructions follow the table.

3.1 Views

When you click **View** on the Ribbon, you are given a number of choices that affect how your document appears on the screen. **Draft** is useful when you are interested in seeing only the text, but not the headers, footers, blank areas, or figures (images or graphs imported into the document). If you want a more realistic view of what the page will look like with headers, footers, blank areas, and figures, then use the **Print Layout** view (this choice is the default).

To see two pages side-by-side, select **View Tab | Zoom | Two Pages**. To edit the header and footer, click **Insert Tab | Header and Footer**. To adjust document size on the screen, click **View Tab | Zoom**. You can type in a percentage, or select an option from the list. Choose a size that makes it easy for you to read the characters on the screen.

3.2 Cut, Copy, and Paste

To use the cut and copy functions, you must first select the text that you want to cut or copy. To select a word, double-click it. To select a paragraph, triple-click anywhere within the paragraph. To select a block of text, use one of the methods described in Section 2.7. Then click either the **Cut** button [insert cut icon here] or the **Copy** button [insert copy icon here] on **Home Tab | Clipboard** or use the keyboard shortcuts Ctrl+X (cut) or Ctrl+C (copy). Move the cursor to where you want to paste this text. It can be pasted into the same document or into another document. Click the **Paste** button [insert paste button here] or use Ctrl+V. Take the time to get used to these shortcuts; they will save you time in the long run.

3.3 Find and Replace

Sometimes you realize that you have been using the wrong word or wrong symbol, or consistently misspelling a word, throughout a paper. This error can be easily remedied using the **Replace** option. Click **Home Tab | Editing | Replace** on the Ribbon. Type in the wrong word next to **Find what**, and the correction next to **Replace with**. If you are *absolutely certain* that you want the change to be made *every time* it appears in the document, then select **Replace all**. If the "wrong word" may not be wrong every time, select **Find next**. This allows you to preview the sentence in which the word was used and gives you the option *not* to replace it in every instance. Be very careful with the Replace All. It is extremely important that you read over your entire paper after you have done this to avoid embarrassing situations and/or bad grades.

When you write the first draft of a paper, you may want to get all your ideas out first, without worrying about details or accuracy. It is important in subsequent drafts, however, to get the facts straight. You should devise your own way of marking the text that needs special attention. For example, you might type **??** after such text. Then when you want to go back and revise these sentences, you simply click **Editing | Find**, and type in **??**.

3.4 Spelling and Grammar

There is absolutely no excuse for typos when Word offers you so many options for checking spelling and grammar:

- AutoCorrect
- Automatic spelling and grammar checker
- Manual, systematic spelling and grammar check

AutoCorrect. The AutoCorrect function corrects common types of spelling mistakes as you type. To see the list of commonly misspelled words that Word corrects automatically, click **Office Button | Word Options | Proofing | AutoCorrect Options**, and scroll through the words on the Auto-Correct tab. If you do not want AutoCorrect to change a particular keystroke combination (e.g., do not change (c) to ©), select this combination on the list and click the **Delete** button. You can also add words that you know you misspell frequently to the list.

If AutoCorrect changes text that you don't want changed while you are typing, click **Undo** on the Quick Access Toolbar or just press Ctrl+Z after the change.

Automatic spelling and grammar checker. The automatic spelling and grammar checker underlines in red the words that are not in Word's spelling dictionary, and underlines in green possible grammatical errors.

To deal with a word underlined in red, click it with the *right* mouse button. A pop-up menu appears with commands and suggestions for replacements (Figure A1.10). Select the correct spelling after you have confirmed the correct spelling in your textbook or laboratory manual. The red under-

Insert a cuvette into the spectrophotometer.

curette
corvette
cavetti
coveted
cavetto
Ignore All
Add to Dictionary
AutoCorrect ▶
Language ▶
Spelling...
Look Up...
Cut
Copy
Paste

Figure A1.10 Dialog box for spelling suggestions and other ways to handle words not in Word's dictionary.

line is deleted, and the word is ignored in the manual, systematic spelling, and grammar check.

To deal with a possible grammatical error underlined in green, click it with the *right* mouse button. A pop-up menu appears (Figure A1.11).

To tell Word how aggressively to check spelling and grammar as you type, click **Office Button | Word Options | Proofing**. Check the boxes of the options you want. For example, under you might check:

- Check spelling as you type
- Always suggest corrections
- Ignore words in uppercase
- Ignore words with numbers
- Ignore Internet and file addresses

Under Grammar, you might select the following options:

- Check grammar as you type
- Check grammar with spelling

When you click the **Settings** box, you have the opportunity to select various grammar and style options.

Manual, systematic spelling and grammar check. To do a manual, systematic spelling and grammar check at any time, click **Review Tab | Spelling and Grammar**. The checker begins at the position of the cursor, and stops at every location at which it doesn't recognize a word or sentence construction. You then have the option of changing the word/construction, ignoring it, or adding the word to Word's dictionary. When the spell checker stops at a scientific word, consult your textbook for the correct spelling, as specialized terminology is not included in Word's dictionary.

The egg white sample were serially diluted.

	sample was
	samples were
	Ignore Once
	Grammar...
	About This Sentence
	Look Up...
	Cut
	Copy
	Paste

Figure A1.11 Dialog box for editing possible grammatical errors.

As good as these features are, remember that **a spell checker is no substitute for a human proofreader**. Spell checkers cannot recognize all mistakes of misuse, such as *you're* and *your*, and they are not familiar with expressions such as *pH*. In fact, the spell checker may even try to get you to change a proper scientific word to a word in its repertoire that obviously makes no sense. Be vigilant and use common sense!

3.5 Word Count

The length of your lab report or paper depends on the detail expected by your instructor. Most instructors prefer not to specify a page length, stating simply that the work should be complete and concise. As a general rule, shorter is better.

If you do honors or graduate research later on, you may be expected to submit a proposal of a certain length. If the specifications are given in terms of words, the word count feature is helpful. Click **Review Tab | Proofing | Word Count**, and Word will tally the number of words in the document. Word also keeps track of the word count at the bottom left of the Word window.

3.6 Tracking Changes Made By Peer Reviewers

It may not always be possible for you and your peer reviewer to find a common time to go over your paper. E-mail makes the peer review process more convenient. You can send your paper to your peer reviewer in electronic format as an attached file, your peer reviewer can make comments directly in your file, and then the reviewer can send it back to you.

It is important for you to be able to distinguish your original text from the comments and changes suggested by your peer reviewer. After all, *you* are the author, and you have the right to accept or decline a reviewer's suggestions.

Before you send your lab report to a peer reviewer, click **Review Tab | Track Changes**. As long as this box is selected, anything someone types in the document will be underlined and be in a colored font. Anything someone deletes will be crossed out and be in a colored font.

When you get your peer-reviewed document back, open it and read through your reviewer's changes. You can then **Accept or Reject Changes** by pressing the appropriate button in the **Review Tab | Changes** box or simply right click on the change and use the menu that pops up. The **Next** button will take you to the locations where changes were made, and then you can accept or reject them.

To see which reviewer made changes in your text, hold the cursor over the change for a second to display the ScreenTip showing the author, date and time, and type of change.

Make sure to print out the revised version of your paper, and proof-read the hard copy. Some mistakes are more easily identified on paper, and it is always better for you, rather than your instructor, to find them. Also be careful with the way Word signals that a change has been made. You'll notice that changes are marked with a vertical bar on the left side of the text. This line indicates that a reviewer has changed something and it will stay there until you accept or reject that change. Sometimes it is easy to miss a change, but the bar will still be there to indicate that you should go back and view it.

4. Special Functions in Scientific Papers

Scientific papers possess features that are usually not found in papers written in the humanities. These include:

- Greek letters and mathematical symbols
- Superscripts and subscripts
- Italics to indicate the scientific name of an organism
- Tables inserted in the document
- Figures imported from another program such as Excel
- Equations

In addition, you may need to leave space in order to add hand-drawn sketches to your paper. Another spacing requirement is hanging indents, which are used to separate references in name-year format. You can use the Quick Reference Table (Table A1.3) if you are already familiar with these features.

4.1 Greek Letters and Mathematical Symbols

In the past, some instructors may have allowed you to write Greek letters and mathematical symbols in by hand. The problem with this approach is that it is easy to miss one of the places where these characters should be inserted in your text, and this oversight may cost you points on your grade. Furthermore, handwritten characters make the paper look unprofessional. Take some time to locate the symbols you need before you write your paper.

1. Click the **Insert Tab | Symbols group | Symbol** on the Ribbon.
2. If the symbol you are looking for isn't in the pop up menu, select **More Symbols**, then **Font:** (normal text) and browse the available characters in this character set (Figure A1.12). You will find commonly used scientific symbols such as:

Symbol	Meaning
°	degree(s)
±	plus or minus
μ	micron (10–6 m)
‰	parts per thousand
f	function (calculus)

In the Normal text character set, you will also find characters with diacritical marks used in European languages other than English. Some common letters with diacritical marks are:

Name	Example
Accent	À, Á, È, É, Ì, Í, Ò, Ó, Ù, Ú, à, á, è, é, ò, ó, ì, í, ù, ú
Circumflex	Â, Ê, Î, Ô, Û, â, ê, î, ô, û
Cedilla	Ç, ç
Tilde	Ã, Ñ, Õ, ã, ñ, õ
Umlaut	Ä, Ë, Ï, Ö, Ü, Ÿ, ä, ë, ï, ö, ü, ÿ

When you change the Font to Symbol (see Figure A1.12), you will find upper- and lowercase Greek letters and other symbols used in mathematics and chemistry such as:

Symbol	Meaning
≤,≥	is less than or equal to, is greater than or equal to
∞	infinity
•	raised period (centered dot); multiplication symbol in equations; connection for adducts in a chemical formula
→,←,↔	arrows used to write chemical reactions
∂	partial derivative (calculus)

3. Once you have found the letter or symbol you need, simply click it and select the **Insert** button at the bottom of the dialog box.

If you use a Greek letter or mathematical symbol frequently, you can make a shortcut key to save time (see Section 4.5).

TABLE A1.3 Quick reference for features used in scientific papers

FEATURE	QUICK REFERENCE
Greek letters	Insert Tab | Symbols Group | Symbol
	Choose a Font: (normal text) or Symbol
Mathematical symbols	Insert Tab | Symbols Group | Symbol
	Choose a Font: (normal text) or Symbol. Mathematical Operators is a choice in the Subset drop down menu in the Symbol Dialog Box.
Superscripts and subscripts	Home Tab | Font | Superscript or Subscript buttons
	Keyboard shortcuts: Ctrl + (Subscript); Ctrl + Shift + (Superscript)
Italics	I button in Home Tab | Font
	Keyboard shortcut: Ctrl + I
Customize toolbar (Quick Access Toolbar only)	Office Button | Word Options | Customize
	This will allow you to add buttons to the Quick Access Toolbar. You cannot customize the Ribbon.
Shortcut keys	Insert Tab | Symbols | Symbol | More Symbols Select a character, then click the Shortcut Key button to assign a keystroke combination for that symbol
AutoCorrect	Office Button | Word Options | Proofing | AutoCorrect Options
Tables inserted in the document	Insert Tab | Tables | Table
Figures imported from another program such as Excel	See Appendix 2
Equations	Insert Tab | Equation
	Note: You may need to install Microsoft Equation 3.0 to be able to use this function. It is found on the installation CD for Office 2007.
Measuring space	Word processor's ruler
Hanging indent to list references	Home Tab | Paragraph | Corner Icon | Indents and Spacing tab | Indentation: Special | Hanging

Figure A1.12 Symbol dialog box showing characters under Font: (normal text).

4.2 Superscripts and Subscripts

Some expressions used in the natural sciences have superscripted or subscripted characters. It is *not correct* to write these characters on the same line as the rest of the text. Similarly, when using scientific notation, exponents are always superscripted. It is *not acceptable* to write exponents preceded by a caret ($\wedge$) or by an uppercase E to designate superscript; these conventions have evolved for use in documents such as electronic mail in which formatting is not available. Do not use them in a printed paper.

> **RIGHT:** 2×10^{-1} (exponent is superscripted)
> **WRONG:** $2 \times 10–3$ or $2 \times 10^\wedge–3$ or $2 \times 10E–3$

To superscript or subscript text:

1. Type the expression without superscripting or subscripting.
2. Select the character(s) to be sub- or superscripted.
3. Click **Home Tab | Font | Corner Icon** on the Ribbon.
4. Check the appropriate box under **Effects** in the **Font** dialog box (Figure A1.13).
5. Click **OK**. The text you selected is formatted.

Figure A1.13 Font dialog box.

Alternatively, you can apply sub- and superscripting using keyboard commands. Select the character(s), then press Ctrl+ for subscript, or Ctrl + Shift+ for superscript.

4.3 Italics

By convention, scientific names given to organisms (viruses, bacteria, plants, and animals) are in Latin and are written in italics, with the genus name capitalized and the species name lowercase (e.g. *Pinus rigida* for pitch pine). After you type the name of the organism, select it and click the *I* button on the **Home Tab** | **Font** group. However, it is much easier to just press Ctrl + I.

If you have to type certain scientific names frequently, use AutoCorrect (see Section 4.6) either to replace the name with a simple keystroke combination or to have it italicized automatically.

4.4 Customizing Your Toolbars

After you have used Word for a while, you may notice that you frequently use commands that are buried deep in the Ribbon. In Word 2003, you could customize all of your toolbars that appeared at the top of the screen. In Word 2007, you are only allowed to customize the Quick Access Toolbar and not any part of the Ribbon.

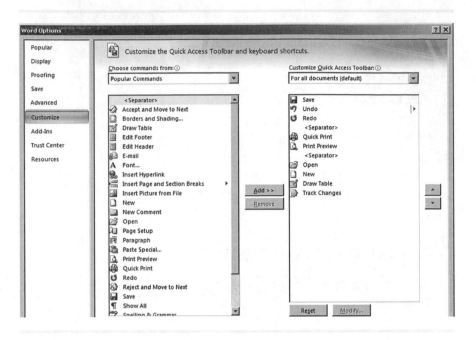

Figure A1.14 Customize dialog box.

Adding commands to the Quick Access toolbar. You can add frequently used commands, such as Undo and Print to the Quick Access Toolbar. To do this:

1. Click **Office Button | Word Options | Customize** from the options dialog box

2. The left side shows different categories, such as File, Edit, View and the other categories from the Ribbon. The right side shows the commands in the order they will appear in the Quick Access Toolbar (Figure A1.14).

3. Click the button you'd like to add to the toolbar from the left menu. Click **Add** (in the middle), then you can adjust the order by clicking the up and down arrows on the far right.

If you use Word a lot, it may be worth your while to browse the categories and commands in the **Customize** dialog box. Make frequently used commands more accessible by adding them to the toolbar or menu bar. This is an especially convenient feature if you miss the way Word 2003 was laid out. You can at least keep a few of the functions you use most often always visible on the screen.

4.5 Shortcut Keys

It is very time-consuming to go through the **Insert Tab | Symbols | Symbol | More Symbols | ChooseFont | Click symbol | Click Insert** routine every time you want to insert a degree sign in your paper. It is worth your while to make shortcut keys for frequently used symbols. To do this, go to **Insert Tab | Symbols | Symbol | More Symbols** click the desired symbol. Notice the **Shortcut Key** button at the bottom of the **Symbol** dialog box (see Figures A1.12). When you click this button, you have the opportunity to define a combination of keystrokes for that particular symbol (Figure A1.15). The combination should be easy to remember and is usually Ctrl, Alt, Ctrl+Shift, or Ctrl+Alt plus some other character.

Let's say you want to make a shortcut key for the degree sign. The degree sign looks like a lowercase *o*, so you might use Alt+o. You type Alt+o into the **Press new shortcut key** box, and Word notifies you either that this combination is unassigned (as in Figure A1.15) or that it has already been

Figure A1.15 Customize Keyboard dialog box.

assigned to another command. (*Note:* Even though you typed Alt and a lowercase *o*, the shortcut appears as Alt and uppercase *O* in the box. If you had typed Alt and uppercase *O*, this would have appeared as Alt+Shift+O.)

If the shortcut is already assigned to a different command, determine if you use that command very often. If you don't, you can remove the shortcut from the seldom-used command and assign it to the symbol you want. To do this:

1. Select **Assign** from the buttons at the bottom of the dialog box (see Figure A1.15). Alt+o will then be listed under **Current keys**. If Word assigned a different shortcut key to the degree sign, this will also be displayed under **Current keys** (in this example, Ctrl+ , Space).

2. Click the previously assigned shortcut key, and then select **Remove** from the buttons at the bottom of the dialog box.

3. Close the **Customize Keyboard** dialog box.

4. Close the **Symbol** dialog box.

Next time you have to write the symbol for "degrees Celsius," simply type Alt+o followed by uppercase *C* to get: °C.

4.6 AutoCorrect

AutoCorrect is useful for more than just correcting spelling mistakes. Four possible applications in scientific writing are:

- To replace long chemical names with a simple keystroke combination
- To insert symbols or special characters using just one keyboard key
- To italicize scientific names of organisms automatically
- To insert expressions with sub- or superscripts automatically

Replacing long chemical names with a simple keystroke combination. It is tedious to type units and long chemical names that occur frequently in your text. To save yourself some keystrokes, you can program AutoCorrect to replace an expression that takes a long time to type with a simple keystroke combination. You must choose the simple keystroke combination judiciously, however, because every time you type these keystrokes, Word will replace them with what you programmed in AutoCorrect. One "trick" is to precede the keystroke combination with either a comma or semicolon (, or ;). Since these punctuation marks are typically followed by a space and not a letter, adding one before your "code letter(s)" creates a unique combination.

For example, let's say "beta-galactosidase" is a word you have to type frequently. You choose ";bg" to designate "beta-galactosidase." To program **AutoCorrect** for this entry:

1. Select **Office Button | Word Options | Proofing | AutoCorrect** (you could also right click on ";bg" to bring up a menu that features AutoCorrect). This opens the **AutoCorrect** dialog box.

2. Type ";bg" in the **Replace** text box.

3. Type "beta-galactosidase" in the **With** text box.

4. Click the **Add** button.

5. Click **OK**.

Inserting symbols or special characters using just one keyboard key. If you want to use AutoCorrect to insert symbols or special characters, the procedure is as follows:

1. Select **Insert Tab | Symbols | Symbol | More Symbols** from the Ribbon. This opens the **Symbol** dialog box (see Figure A1.12).

2. Change the font if the symbol you want to use is not in the (normal text) font.

3. Click the symbol.

4. Click the **AutoCorrect** button at the bottom of the dialog box. The symbol will already be entered in the **With** text box.

5. In the **Replace** text box, type the characters you want to replace with the symbol.

6. Click the **Add** button.

7. Click **OK**.

Italicizing scientific names of organisms automatically. If you are going to be typing the scientific name of an organism repeatedly, you can insure that it always appears in italics without manually imposing italics each time. To do this, follow these steps:

1. First type the scientific name of the organism in your text (e.g., Aphanizomenon flos-aquae).

2. Italicize the name by selecting it and then clicking the **Italicize** button (*I*) in **Home Tab | Font** or typing the keyboard command Ctrl+I; either way, the text should become *Aphanizomenon flos-aquae*.

3. With the name still selected, click **Office Button | Word Options | Proofing | AutoCorrect** (you could also right click on the word and choose AutoCorrect from the pop-up menu.

4. On the **AutoCorrect** tab, you will notice Aphanizomenon already entered in the **With** text box. Click the **Formatted text** option button to italicize it.

5. Enter a shorter version of the name in the **Replace** text box, for example "aphan."

6. Click the **Add** button.

7. Click **OK** to close the window.

Inserting expressions with sub- and superscripts. The principle of using AutoCorrect to insert expressions with sub- and superscripts is the same as that for italicizing scientific names.

1. Type the expression without sub- or superscripts (e.g., Vmax).

2. Select the characters to be sub- or superscripted, and then format them as described in Section 4.2 or 4.4 (the expression becomes V_{max}).

3. Select the entire expression, and click **Office Button | Word Options | Proofing | AutoCorrect** (alternately, you could right click on the expression and select AutoCorrect options from there).

4. On the AutoCorrect tab, you will notice "V_{max}" already entered in the **With** text box. Click the **Formatted Text** option to add the subscripting.

5. Type "Vmax" in the **Replace** text box.

6. Click the **Add** button.

7. Click **OK** to close the window.

4.7 Tables Inserted in the Document

Tables may be inserted as soon as feasible following the text where the table is first mentioned. Most people find it easier to refer to a table that is in close proximity to the text.

Word makes it easy to create tables to your specifications (see Section 2.12). You can also make tables in Excel (see "Importing Tables From Excel Into a Word Document" in Appendix 2), and then import and format them in Word (see below).

4.8 Figures Imported from Another Program Such as Excel

The general idea behind importing figures from another program into Word is:

1. Activate the desired graphic.

2. Click the **Copy** button on the Standard toolbar (or **Edit | Copy** on the menu bar or Ctrl + C) in the graphing program.

3. Position the cursor at the location in the Word document where you would like to insert the graphic.

4. Click the **Paste** button on the **Home Tab | Clipboard | Paste** on the Ribbon or Ctrl + V in Word.

To import a graph (figure) from Excel, follow these steps:

1. First you must make the graph in Excel (see Appendix 2). **Make all formatting changes in Excel,** as it is not possible to make any changes (except to the size) once the graph has been imported into your Word document.

2. When you are satisfied with the graph in Excel, single-click the area outside the axex, but inside the frame (**Chart Area**, not **Plot Area**).

3. Click the **Copy** button on the **Home Tab | Clipboard** or press Ctrl + C or right click to copy the graph to the clipboard.

4. Return to your Word document and position the cursor at the desired location.

5. Click the **Paste** button on the Word **Home Tab | Clipboard** or press Ctrl + V or right click.

6. The figure will appear in the Word document.

7. Type a figure caption **below** the figure. The caption consists of the word "Figure" followed by a number and descriptive title. Center the caption or align it flush on the left margin. Use Arabic numbers and number the figures consecutively in the order they are described in the text.

8. Figure titles should be informative and consist of a precise noun phrase (not a complete sentence). Titles that merely state the y-axis legend versus the x-axis legend are not acceptable.

4.9 Equations

It is unlikely that you will need to type complex mathematical equations in a scientific paper for an introductory biology course. If you are interested in doing so, however, you can open Microsoft Equation Editor by selecting **Insert Tab | Equation. Microsoft Equation 3.0** may need to be loaded onto your computer; it can be found on the Office 2007 Installation CD. Several references in the Bibliography provide instructions.

4.10 Importing Figures into Word

In some laboratory exercises, you may be asked to include a picture or diagram of what you've done. You may also be asked to sketch cells, tissue sections, or specimens that you viewed under the microscope. By convention, these sketches are called "figures" and require a figure caption (number and title) beneath the figure.

If you have a sketch, we recommend scanning it and saving it as an image file (.jpg, .tif, .png, etc.). Photos and scanned images can then be imported into Word. Follow these steps:

1. Go to **Insert Tab | Illustrations | Picture**.

2. In the dialog box that opens up, find where you saved your image, and open it.

3. The image will then be imported into Word. This makes the **Picture Tools Tab** appear. You can use the options available there to resize, crop, and arrange the image.

Your figure will then need a name (Figure 1, Figure 2, etc.) and a short explanation of what is displayed in the figure. You can insert a text box by going to **Insert Tab | Text | Text Box**. The figure and the caption should be aligned with the nearest side of the figure (for example, if the caption is under the figure, it should be aligned with the left side of the figure). In Word 2003, this was a simple task requiring only a right click on the selected objects to be aligned; you could even group the text box and figure together and move them around at the same time. Now, in Word 2007, things are more complicated. There is no easy way to group objects that are of different types. To align or group your figure and caption, you must first create what is called a "Drawing Canvas."

1. Go to **Insert Tab | Illustrations | Shapes | New Drawing Canvas**

2. Cut and paste your figure and text box into the drawing canvas.

3. You can then group or align them by holding down the Ctrl button and selecting both with your mouse and going to **Picture Tools Format Tab | Arrange | Align or Group**. Remember, this tab is only visible when you have a picture selected.

4.11 Hanging Indent to List References in the Name-Year System

The Council of Science Editors (CSE Manual 2006) recommends two formats for listing references, the Citation-Sequence System and the Name-Year System (see Chapter 4, pp. 59–63).

If you use the Citation-Sequence system, the references are numbered according to order of citation. See Section 2.13 of this appendix for instructions on how to make numbered lists.

If you use the Name-Year system, the references are listed in alphabetical order according to the first author's last name. The first line of the reference begins on the left margin, and the subsequent lines are indented. This style is called a **hanging indent**. References typed with hanging indent format look like this:

Murata T, Kadota A, Wada M. 1997. Effects of blue light on cell elongation and microtubule orientation in dark-grown gametophytes of *Ceratopteris richardii*. Plant and Cell Physiology 38(2):201–209.

There are several ways to apply hanging indent format to the list of references. Perhaps the easiest is to type each reference so that it is aligned on the left margin, with an **Enter** (Return) at the end of each reference. When you are finished, select all the references (see Section 2.7), and then click **Home Tab | Paragraph | Corner Icon** on the Ribbon. On the **Indents and Spacing** tab (see Figure A1.6), scroll down to **Hanging** in the **Indentation: Special** box. You can set the indentation to 0.25" or 0.5" in the **By:** box.

DATA MANAGEMENT IN MICROSOFT EXCEL

Collecting data and creating graphs are characteristic of the scientific process and scientific and technical writing. They help the reader to visualize the data, and to see relationships among variables. Graphs are a way to summarize information that would otherwise involve lengthy descriptions that would be difficult to interpret.

Years ago, authors used drawing instruments, specially lined graph paper, and ink to make figures for published papers. Mistakes were difficult, if not impossible to correct, so any mistake usually resulted in starting over. If a different sized figure was required, the entire figure had to be redrawn. The advent of plotting software in the mid-1980s, however, has made hand-drawn graphs practically obsolete. You simply enter the data into a graphics program in a prescribed manner and select the desired form for the graph; the computer draws the graph for you.

The most common types of graphs used in introductory biology courses are **line graphs**, **scatter plots**, **bar graphs**, and **histograms**. The type of graph you choose should be based on which one best depicts and emphasizes the trends shown by your data. Some guidelines for helping you choose an appropriate type of graph are given in Chapter 4.

This appendix will take you from data entry and organization to basic statistical analysis to the creation of graphs in Microsoft Excel 2007. Excel is a good plotting program for novices for the following reasons:

- Data input and subsequent plotting of these data is relatively straightforward in Excel.

- Excel is readily available and is included in Microsoft Office.

- If your school has Excel on its computers, it's likely that you can get assistance from a staff member in your school's computer services department.

The time you invest now in learning to plot data on the computer will be invaluable in your upper-level courses and later in your career. You may eventually switch to a higher-powered plotting program such as SigmaPlot, but the experience gained by working with Excel should make this transition easier.

The format described in this appendix is the format that we suggest that you use for your laboratory reports for introductory biology. Instructions to "single-click" or "double-click" refer to clicking the *left* mouse button, unless otherwise noted.

The screen drops in this appendix are for Excel 2007. Be advised: the instructions probably will not apply to earlier versions due to the way in which Microsoft has changed the once-familiar program. Excel commands are distinguished in this appendix with a vertical bar, separating commands from subcommands. For example, **Home tab | Font | Corner Icon** means "Click the Home tab (on the Ribbon), then find the Font group, and then click the icon in the corner to open the Font Dialog Box."

1. The Microsoft Excel Screen

Open an Excel worksheet (spreadsheet). A worksheet consists of thousands of cells arranged in rows and columns, with the Ribbon located above the cells at the top of the screen display (Figure A2.1). The columns have letter headings (A, B, C, etc.) and the rows have numerical headings (1, 2, 3, etc.).

1.1 Title bar

The title of the worksheet is given at the very top of the page on a blue background. If you have not yet named the worksheet, the title bar will read Microsoft Excel—Book 1.

Figure A2.1 Screen display of Excel 2007 worksheet with the Ribbon at the top of the window.

Excel 2007 Update

The Microsoft Office 2007 programs look different from their predecessors. The new default window features the Ribbon above the worksheet space (see Figure A2.1). The Office Button is at the top left corner of the window. This button contains many items that used to be contained in the File Menu. Next to the Office Button at the top of the page is the Quick Access Toolbar. You can customize this toolbar by adding buttons for commands that you use most often. To do this, click **Office Button | Excel Options | Customize**. You can then choose which buttons to add by finding them in the left-hand menu and adding them to the right.

1.2 The Ribbon

Like other Office 2007 programs, the Ribbon is prominently displayed at the top of your window. The Ribbon contains all of the functions that were formerly organized in toolbars and menus. In Excel 2007, the Ribbon groups commands by general categories in tabs and more specific related functions in groups within each tab. If you are used to Office 2003, it may take you a while to find everything in this new scheme.

When you place the mouse pointer over a particular button on the Ribbon (do not click any mouse buttons), a description of that button will appear.

1.3 Formula bar

The formula bar is located just below the Ribbon. It is used to enter formulas for performing calculations on the data entered in the spreadsheet. It is also used to edit the contents of a cell. You can also do this editing directly in the cell.

2. Entering Data into a Spreadsheet

2.1 Organization and Formatting

The first thing you should do when you acquire new data is enter them into a program that will allow you to organize and analyze them. For our purposes in introductory biology, we are using Excel. It helps if you have a clear idea of what your XY graph should look like before you enter data. Which parameter should be plotted on the x-axis and which one on the y-axis? By convention, the x-axis of the graph shows the independent variable. The **independent variable** is the one that the scientist manipulated during the experiment. The y-axis of the graph shows the dependent variable. The **dependent variable** is the measured variable and typically changes in response to the independent variable.

Let's say you conducted an experiment in which you determined how the activity of an enzyme (catalase) changed when you varied the temperature. Because you manipulated the temperature in the experiment, it is the independent variable and should be plotted on the x-axis. Enzyme activity is the dependent variable because it changes in response to changes in the temperature, and should be plotted on the y-axis. For a non-biological example, imagine you are firing a cannon and measuring where the cannon ball lands. The angle of the cannon barrel is the independent variable because it is what you are manipulating and should be plotted on the x-axis. The distance that the cannon ball travels is the measured variable, or dependent variable, and should be plotted on the y-axis. The dependent variable (the distance that the cannon ball travels) is a result of the change in the independent variable (the angle of the cannon barrel).

On the Excel spreadsheet, **Column A** is used to enter the data for the x**-axis**, whereas subsequent columns are used for data for the y**-axis** (Table A2.1). In the enzyme example, temperature data is plotted in Column A and the corresponding catalase activity data is plotted in Column B.

Enter the data as in Table A2.1. For a simple graph with only one data set, it is not necessary to provide column headings. If you need column headings, enter them in the first row. As you become more familiar with Excel, you will see that there are other ways you can enter your data and Excel will still make an appropriate graph, but for our purposes, use these instructions.

You may notice that as you are entering data, Excel does some automatic formatting. For example, if you type in "1.60," Excel removes the last zero. You need to specify how many digits you want to appear in each column. If you want that hundredths digit to appear, highlight the column by clicking on the column letter. Then go to **Home tab | Number**. From here, there are four different ways to adjust the number of decimal places. First, you can click the drop-down menu and select the format style you want from there. Another way is to click the **Increase** or **Decrease Decimal** Button. The third way is to click the **Corner Icon** and then select the style from the dialog box that opens. You can also right-click on the highlighted cells and then choose **Format Cells** from the pop-up menu.

Another note about formatting cells is that there are a number of ways for you to format cells to make them appear to your liking. We recommend playing around with these features, as that is a good way to learn them. In

TABLE A2.1 Sample data for effect of temperature on catalase activity. Temperatures (°C) are entered in Column A, catalase activity (units of product formed · sec^{-1}) in Column B.

	A	B
1	4	0.039
2	11115	0.073
3	223	0.077
4	330	0.096
5	337	0.082
6	5050	0.04
7	660	0.007
8	70	0
9	10100	0

addition to formatting the numbers, as mentioned above, you can change the format of many other aspects of a cell, such as character alignment. You can align characters in cells just as you can do in Word. See **Home tab | Alignment**. You can also make the text go off at angles. If you have a lot to write in a cell, you can click **Wrap Text** to create multiple lines of text in a cell. You can also merge multiple cells into one if you want a common heading over a few separate columns. If you go to **Home tab | Alignment | Corner Icon** you can see what your options are in a dialog box that is much easier to understand than the Ribbon.

2.2 Viewing The Data

Freezing panes. You may have a lot of data to enter that fills up your screen. As you go down the sheet entering the data, the column headings that are in the first row disappear. It is helpful to keep the labels visible as you add data so the data go in the correct column. To keep the first row visible, go to the **View tab | Window | Freeze Panes | Freeze Top Row**. As you can see from the menu that appears, you can also do this with the first column.

Sorting Data. You may also want to sort your data. Let's say you are a teacher and have to calculate your final grades. You may want all students with grades of 90–100 to get an A, 80–89 a B, etc. It would be much more efficient for you to assign the grades if your data were sorted by grade. To

Figure A2.2 Sorting data dialog box

do this, make sure you click once on a cell that has data in it, then go to **Data tab | Sort & Filter | Sort** to open the Sort Dialog box (Figure A2.2). From here you can choose which column to sort by (here, grades). Then sort on "Values" because you want to rank the grades by number, then choose the order you want them to be in.

Page Break Preview. Sometimes you may want to print your data sheets. It helps to be able to see the area that you are printing. To do this, go to **View tab | Workbook Views | Page Break Preview**. In this view, you can move around the page margins and make adjustments to the whole print area.

2.3 Manipulating the Data

In Excel, you can enter equations in the formula bar and the answers will appear in the cell. The formula bar appears just below the Ribbon. Let's go back to our grading example. In our worksheet, Column A is Student Name and each of the next 10 columns represents a quiz worth 10 points. In the last column, we want the total for all points earned from quizzes. Click a cell in that column, then type "=," which signals to Excel that you are typing a formula. Then type "SUM(" and highlight the 10 cells that make up the row of quizzes for a student. The SUM function takes the sum of all values in the selected area. When you are finished highlighting, type ")" and press enter. The sum of quiz grades should appear. Another way of doing this would be to follow the equals sign with the cells to be added individually. Click a cell in the row, followed by "+" then the next cell, then "+," etc.

There are a number of different functions available in Excel. Go to the Excel Help (the button with a "?" on the right) to find a list of them. You could also go to **Formulas tab | Function Library**. The functions are grouped by category here and you can also search them with the **Insert Function Button**. Here are some common ones:

Function	Formula
=AVERAGE(...)	Calculates the mean of values
=RAND()	Enters a random number between 0 & 1
=RANDBETWEEN(x,y)	Enters a random number between x and y
=SQRT(...)	Calculates the square root of a value
=SUM(...)	Calculates the sum of values

Say you want each student's average quiz grade. You wouldn't want to keep typing "=AVG(....)" over and over if you had 1,200 students, and even copying and pasting would take too long. Excel has a very useful feature that allows you to fill in an entire column with the same thing just by highlighting it. So, on the grade sheet in the last column, you would type in "=AVG(" then highlight one student's row of quiz grades, then close parenthesis. Press Enter to see the average. Now, you can highlight the whole column of numbers and press **Ctrl + D** to fill in each row with that formula. Excel is smart enough to realize that you want the formula to be applied to each row, not to just copy the same average all the way down from the page. Excel will also let you fill across rows, if you ever need to do that. Highlight where you want to fill, then click **Home tab | Editing | Fill**. Also, you can select a cell, left-click the bottom right corner of the cell (the black box) and drag to apply that value, formula, or sequence to the cells that are highlighted. Notice that as you drag, a window will appear that will show you what will be placed in the highlighted cell and, when you are finished, an "auto-fill options" icon will appear. Left-click to change the format of the highlighted cells.

2.4 Worksheet Maintenance

If you are working with multiple data sets, it is important that you keep track of your data. If your data are all from the same experiment (say you have temperature readings, light readings, and plant height all from the same experimental field plot), then you might want to keep all the data together in one file. However, you may want to place each type of data on a separate worksheet. There are tabs at the bottom of the screen (Sheet 1, Sheet 2, and Sheet 3) that can be re-named by right-clicking on them. Use these to keep your data organized. You can also add more sheets to the file by clicking the Insert Worksheet button next to the sheet tabs.

3. Some Basic Data Analysis

Excel has a statistical analysis capability. It is enough for the kinds of analyses you'll need to do in an introductory biology course. In this section, we will review some of the basic kinds of analyses you can run in Excel.

3.1 Descriptive Statistics

Descriptive statistics are used to summarize and describe the location and dispersion of your data. These are things like the mean, median, and mode, which give location information, and the variance and standard deviation, which are measures of the spread of your data. Excel makes it simple to calculate these statistics. Begin typing in the formula. When you get to the open parenthesis, select the cells or column of data you wish to calculate the statistic on. Follow the table below:

Descriptive Statistic	Formula in Excel
Mean	=AVG(x,y,z....)
Median	=MEDIAN(x,y,z...)
Mode	=MODE(x,y,z...)
Variance	=VAR(x,y,z...)
Standard Deviation	=STDEV(x,y,z...)

Alternately, you can get a quick summary of these descriptive statistics with the Analysis ToolPak. (Well, it's quick once you find out where the Add-In is located.) Go to **Office Button | Excel Options | Add-Ins**. You will then see a menu of Add-Ins, separated by whether or not they are active. At the bottom of the window, go to **Manage | Excel Add-ins | Go** to see a list of the inactive add-ins that you can make active. Check the box that says **Analysis ToolPak** and click **OK**. This action makes the Analysis Group appear in the Data tab of the Ribbon. Click on that and you will get a dialog box listing the kinds of statistics you can run (Figure A2.3). Select **Descriptive Statistics** and click **OK**.

The following dialog box will open (Figure A2.4). Click the button in the **Input Range** to highlight the values you want to run your statistics on. If there are labels in the first row, indicate that by checking off that box. Check off the **Summary Statistics** box, then click **OK**. A new worksheet will open up (you can change where the output goes in the output options) displaying a list of descriptive statistics, such as those described above, as well as a few others. Once you have the Analysis ToolPak loaded, these tools do save time.

3.2 Student's t-test

The Student's t-test is a type of statistical hypothesis testing where you are comparing two statistics to see if they are different. They can be two means

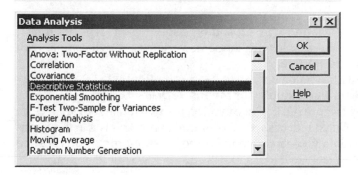

Figure A2.3 Analysis ToolPak dialog box

from two experiments or a hypothesized value and an experimental value. Usually the t-test is done when sample sizes are small, and you can assume that there is a Normal distribution of data. Here again you can do this test in a formula or through a dialog box. The formula you would type in is **=TTEST(array1,array2,tails,type)**, where array1 and array2 are the two

Figure A2.4 Descriptive statistics dialog box

columns of data you are comparing the means of, tails specifies the number of tails in the distribution (1 or 2) and type specifies the type of t-test (1, 2, or 3 for paired, two-sample with the same variance, or two-sample with unequal variance, respectively).

To do a t-test with a dialog box, go to **Data tab | Analysis | Data Analysis | t-test: Paired Two Sample for Means**. A Dialog Box opens that looks like the following (Figure A2.5); you can select the two ranges of variables by highlighting them in your data sheet. If your null hypothesis is that the means are not different, then you enter 0 in the **Hypothesized Mean Difference** box and click **OK**. A table that looks like the one below should appear.

	Variable 1	Variable 2
Mean	13.38889	15.22222
Variance	18.95752	16.06536
Observations	18	18
Pearson Correlation	0.11273	
Hypothesized Mean Difference	0	
Df	17	
t Stat	-1.39502	
P(T<=t) one-tail	0.090485	
t Critical one-tail	1.739607	
P(T<=t) two-tail	0.180971	
t Critical two-tail	2.109816	

Figure A2.5 t-Test: Paired two sample for means

The means of both data ranges are displayed in the first line, followed by their variances, then the number of observations. The rest of the lines give information about the data sets together. The Pearson Correlation gives you r, the product moment correlation, which is the extent to which there is a linear relationship between the two datasets. We entered 0 for the Hypothesized Mean Difference because the null hypothesis is that there is no difference between the means. The degrees of freedom, df, here is 17 because we have 18 observations. The degrees of freedom represent the number of independent observations available to estimate a population parameter (like the mean). The t-Stat is what we are interested in; the probability of this t-value is something you could look up in a statistics text. Fortunately, Excel provides these values in the output so you don't have to look them up. These are P(T<=t) one-tail and P(T<=t) two-tail and the one you use depends on your hypothesis. Excel also gives you the values that your t-Stat requires in order for the difference between the means to be specific at the $\alpha = 0.05$ level. These are the t-Criticals. Here for a one-tailed t-test, the absolute value of our t-statistic needs to be about 1.74, which it is not, so the means between the two groups are not significantly different.

A common mistake made by students is to perform a bunch of t-tests to compare more than two means. This test is inappropriate for that application. What the student should do is an Analysis of Variance, or ANOVA, which is a common statistical procedure used to determine if there are differences between a group of means. You will learn about ANOVA from your statistics courses. ANOVA is included in the Analysis ToolPak of Excel (**Data tab** | **Analysis** | **Data Analysis** | **ANOVA**). For the purposes of introductory biology, you will probably not need to use ANOVA.

3.3 Chi-Square, X^2

The Chi-Square test is used to compare observed and expected values from an experiment. Suppose we are looking at sex ratio in fruit flies, *Drosophila*. Our flies lay 200 eggs; 80 are male and 120 are female. We know that there is a 50% chance of an offspring being male or female. So our expected number of males and females is 100 each. That is not what we got, so how do we tell if our observed result of 80 males and 120 females is just a random chance difference or if there are some other factors at work that affect the sex ratio? We perform a chi-square test. There are other sources that go into detail about calculating a X^2 statistic by hand, so we won't go into that here (though it's pretty easy). Instead, here is how to do it in Excel. First, it is important to have your data entered into your spreadsheet in a way that Excel understands. This means that you need to have one column for observed values and one for your expected (hypothesized) values. Here is what we would enter for our *Drosophila* example:

	observed	expected
male	80	100
female	120	100

The formula you need for the chi-square test is "=CHITEST(actual range, expected range), where "actual range" is your column of observed values and "expected range" is the column of expected values. Type "=CHITEST(" , then highlight the first column, type a comma, then highlight the second column and close the parentheses and press enter. This command returns the P-value for the chi-square value from your data (it does not report the actual X^2 value). This is the probability that the difference you observed is due to chance random variation. The usual cutoff is 0.05, so any number less than that is indicative of a difference that is *not* due to chance. For our example, the probability is around 0.005, indicating that the difference in the number of males and females is not due to chance, and that there is something else affecting the sex ratio.

3.4 Histograms

Histograms allow you to graphically display frequencies or the proportion of cases that fall into specified categories, called Bins. These bins represent specifically sized ranges of values. Let's use a familiar example of test grades. The grades from an exam are listed in Figure A2.6A in the column labeled "Grade" and a list of bins is to its right. *Note*: an extra column (Bin Size) that is *not* needed by Excel to make the histogram is inserted to clarify what values will be included in each bin. Excel will assume that the size of the bin is any number less than or equal to the value in the cell relative to the previous bin. The "Bin Label" column will be used by Excel to label the final bins on the histogram plot. The tabular output from calculating a histogram in Excel is a two-column table, shown in Figure A2.6B. The frequency of the histogram is plotted on the *y*-axis. Simply, this is the number of occurrences for each bin, or the number of grades in each bin. The "more" row will help you spot any data that has not been included in any of your bins.

Here are the steps to follow to make the histogram:

1. Go to **Data tab | Analysis | Data Analysis** and then select **Histogram** from the dialog box that opens.
2. For Input Range select your data (the grades). For Bin Range select your bin values (the bin column).
3. Select **Chart Output** to see a bar graph representation of your histogram (Figure A2.6C). Alternatively, you might see a table.
4. Right-click on parts of the graph to format axes, titles, etc.

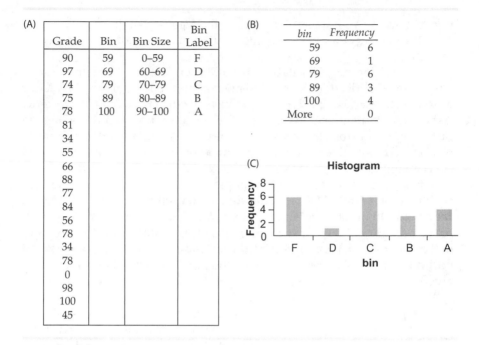

Figure A2.6 Creating a histogram. (A) Format for initial data entry. (B) Tablular output from Histogram analysis. (C) Chart output from Histogram analysis.

See the section on Data Visualization for a guide to formatting charts and graphs.

3.5 Regressions, Correlations, and Trendlines

Trendlines (also called regression lines or "best-fit" lines) are used to look for patterns in a data set and to make predictions about one variable when the other variable is known. Since they are usually associated with a visual output, the description adding these lines can be found in the Data Visualization section below. After you graph your data, Excel allows you to insert a trendline and view the equation for that line. It also reports an R^2 value, which is called the coefficient of determination. R^2 is often confused with R, which is the correlation coefficient. R^2 is the output from a linear regression, where you are looking at how one of your experimental factors influences another factor (say the effect of coffee consumption on heart rate). The R^2 represents the percent of the variance in the data that can be explained by your experimental factor. The correlation coefficient, R, varies between –1 and 1, and the higher its absolute value, the more correlated the two factors are. You can get R by taking the square root of R^2 or by typing "=CORREL(array1,array1)" where array1 is one set of data and array2 is the other set.

If you are looking for a pattern in a data set, first plot the data as a scatter plot (as described in the Data Visualization section). Figure A2.7A, for example, shows class data for a lab exercise in which we would like to know if there is a correlation between caffeine concentration and the change in pulsation rate of blackworms. While there is a significant variation in response for any given caffeine concentration, it looks like a bell-shaped curve might describe the pattern. In Figure A2.7B, a second-order polynomial trendline was fitted to the scatter plot by activating the chart and then clicking **Chart Tools | Layout | Analysis | Trendline** and selecting **More Trendline Options**. In this experiment, the class hypothesizes a second-order polynomial relationship, so choose **Polynomial, 2nd order**, and make sure to click **Display equation on chart** and **Display R-squared value on chart**. The degree to which the trendline actually fits the data is given by the R-squared value, whereby the closer the R-squared value is to 1, the better the correlation or fit. The low R-squared value in this example indicates that the second-order polynomial trendline does not describe the correlation between dose and response very well. We might conclude from these data that caffeine is a stimulant (because pulsation rate mostly increased at all caffeine concentrations tested), but that there is no clear relationship between caffeine concentration and response.

If your objective is to make predictions about one variable when the other is known, you may try to fit a linear trendline to the data set, as for a standard curve. Some examples in biology where standard curves are used include:

- Predicting the protein concentration of an unknown sample using the correlation between absorbance and known protein concentration (e.g., Biuret method, Bradford method). An example of this is below.

- Determining the size of a DNA fragment by comparing the distance it migrated on a gel to the distance migrated by DNA fragments whose sizes are known.

- Quantifying nitrogen or phosphorous in aquatic ecosystems.

Example: Standard Curve for a Protein Assay. Let's say you did an experiment in which you used the Biuret method to determine protein concentration in an egg white. In the first step of the procedure, you measured the absorbance of four known concentrations of bovine serum albumin (BSA) to make the standard curve. Because of Beer's Law, we expect the standard

Figure A2.7 Effect of caffeine on the pulsation rate of blackworms. The percent change was determined by subtracting the rate before treatment from the rate after treatment, dividing by the rate before treatment, and multiplying by 100. (A) Data initially graphed as a scatter plot to look for possible patterns. (B) The same data with a second-order polynomial trendline fitted by Excel. The low R^2 value indicates that this trendline does not describe the correlation between change in pulsation rate and caffeine concentration very well.

TABLE A2.2 Sample data for Biuret standard curve. Protein concentrations (mg/mL) are entered in Column A, absorbance values (at 550 nm) in Column B.

	A	B
1	2	0.10
2	3	0.12
3	5	0.24
4	10	0.40

curve—a graph of absorbance vs. protein concentration—to be a straight line. Follow these steps to plot the standard curve:

1. Enter the BSA concentration in Column A and the corresponding absorbance values in Column B (Table A2.2).

2. Select the cells containing the data and select **Insert tab | Charts | Scatter | No points connected**.Tthe resulting graph should look like Figure A2.8.

3. Select the chart to make it active, then select **Chart Tools | Layout | Analysis | Trendline | Linear Trendline**.

4. Then, from the **Trendline menu** select **More Trendline Options**. Under the Trendline Options menu check the boxes next to **Dis-**

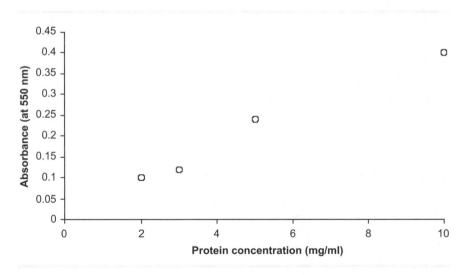

Figure A2.8 Biuret standard curve as a scatter plot. See Figure A2.9 for final form.

Figure A2.9 Biuret standard curve with trendline extrapolated backward to the origin and the equation of the line displayed along with the R^2 value.

play equation on chart and **Display R-squared value**. The equation allows you to predict the concentration in a sample of egg white (the "unknown") when its absorbance is known (measured). The R-squared value tells you how well the equation fits the data.

5. Depending on the sensitivity range of the assay, it may be appropriate to extrapolate the linear trendline backward or forward. To do this, set **Forecast Backward** (or **Forward**) the appropriate number of units under **Trendline Options**. In Figure A2.9, "2" was entered for Forecast Backward.

6. Select **OK**. The resulting figure should look like Figure A2.9. *Note*: If desired, single-click the equation box to change y and x in the equation to the actual symbols for the variables.

7. **To modify an existing trendline**, select the chart and go to **More Trendline Options** again.

4. Data Visualization in Excel

Excel allows you to create graphs and figures based on the data you enter into it. Here is where you will find one of the biggest differences between Excel

TABLE A2.3 Excel-specific terminology

EXCEL TERM	DESCRIPTION
Chart	Graph
Category axis	*x*-axis
Value axis	*y*-axis
Data series	Set of related data points
Plot area	Area of the graph inside the axes
Chart area	Area outside the axes but inside the frame
Legend	Legend or key

2003 and Excel 2007. There is no longer a Chart Wizard to give you a clear, step-by-step process to produce a graph. Now in Excel 2007, you are on your own, navigating the Ribbon to find formerly easy-to-access commands. Follow our guide below to become familiar with this new set-up and you will soon be able to make figures that summarize your data for your lab reports.

The terminology that Excel uses for graphs is different from what biologists use. For example, you have already learned that Excel calls a spreadsheet a worksheet. The Excel instructions provided here use the terms biologists use, rather than those chosen by Excel. It is helpful to know the Excel terminology when you use the Help menus, however, and Table A2.3 translates some common Excel terms into biologists' terms.

4.1 Using Excel's Chart Tools to Plot Your Data

In the spreadsheet, **select the data to be plotted using the mouse**. To do this, single-click the left mouse button on the first cell, and keep holding the button down as you drag the mouse pointer over the rest of the cells that contain the data to be plotted. When you release the mouse button, the cells you selected are highlighted in blue. Alternatively, click the top left box of the block of data, hold down the Shift key, and click the bottom right box of the block. All the selected cells are highlighted in blue.

Note: If the data to be plotted are not in adjacent columns, highlight the first column, hold down the **Ctrl** key, and then highlight the data in any other column(s).

Go to **Charts** under the **Insert tab**. There you will be able to **select the type of plot by clicking on one of the icons** (Figure A2.10). Each icon opens a drop-down menu that has a number of specialized chart sub-types.

- To make a line graph, select **XY (Scatter)** (Figure A2.11). Do *not* select **Line**, because this option spaces the *x*-axis values at equal intervals, instead of according to the intervals of the data.

Figure A2.10 The chart selection group on the ribbon.

- For Chart sub-type, you must decide whether the points should be connected or not (see Chapter 4 for an explanation of these formats). If there are only a few data points, and you want to show the relationship between the independent variable and the dependent variable, then select **Data points connected by smoothed or straight lines**. Usually your instructor wants to see the data points, so do *not* select the options in which Excel plots the curve without displaying the data points. If you are making a standard curve or a scatter plot, then select **Scatter with no points connected**.

Figure A2.11 Selecting a type of graph in Charts from the Insert tab. Current selection is XY Scatter with unconnected data points.

Figure A2.12 Worksheet containing data and its corresponding chart.

A Chart representing the selected data points will appear in your worksheet (Figure A2.12). When the Chart is selected you will have access to a number of **Chart Tools tabs** (Figure A2.13).

- The **Design tab** will allow you to make basic changes to your chart. You can make quick changes to the layout and change the style and color of your data points.

- The **Layout tab** will allow you to make changes to the layout of your chart. You can insert pictures, shapes, or text boxes. The **Labels** box will allow you to edit the Titles, Axis, Gridlines, Legend, and Data Labels. You will probably spend most of your time using this tab from the Ribbon. The best way to become familiar with each option is to make a sample graph and play around with choices.

Chart Tools

| Design | Layout | Format |

Figure A2.13 Chart Tools with formatting options available when chart is activated.

- The **Format tab** allows you to change aspects of the graph that are not directly related to the data. Generally, you want to keep your graphs simple and clear so the reader can quickly understand what you are trying to summarize with your figure.

4.2 Modifying Graphs

Graphs produced by Excel can be modified to meet an instructor's or a journal's specifications. To modify a graph after you've created it, first activate it by single-clicking the plot area or chart area (Figure A2.14). The Chart Tools tabs will appear in the Ribbon. The Chart Tools will be customized depending on what part of the chart you select and wish to modify. If you want to see what the data look like plotted in another form, select **Design | Type | Change Chart Type**. Check with your instructor regarding what chart type is appropriate.

4.3 Graphing Guidelines for Lab Reports

Before we go further with charting options, let's quickly go over some guidelines for including figures in your lab reports:

Figure A2.14 Text Boxes appear and allow you to enter axis titles.

- **Titles: Leave blank** if this graph is for a lab report or poster. By doing so, Excel will make a larger graph for you to import into your text document later. In the text document, type the figure caption *under* the figure. **Add a title** if the graph is for an oral presentation.

- **Value (X) axis:** Select **Chart Tools tab | Layout | Axis Titles | Primary Horizontal Axis Title | Title Below Axis**. A Text box will appear under the X-axis. There you can enter the *x*-axis label with the units in parentheses. For the data in Table A2.1, the *x*-axis label would be: Temperature (°C). Make sure you always include the units of your data in the axis labels.

- **Value (Y) axis:** Select **Chart Tools | Layout | Axis Titles | Primary Vertical Axis Title** and your desired title format from the drop-down menu. Enter the *y*-axis label with the units in parentheses into the Text box on your chart. For the data in Table A2.1, the *y*-axis label would be: Catalase activity (units of product formed • sec^{-1}). In this and any text box, you can insert symbols and superscripts using the formatting options from the **Home tab**.

- **Axes:** For our purposes, no changes to the axes scales are recommended. Usually, Excel uses scales that are appropriate for viewing all of the data. If you want to change them, go to the **Chart Tools | Axes | Axes** drop-down menu, choose your axis, and select **More Options** from the menu. From the dialog box that opens, you can change the range of your axes. You can also change the axes to a logarithmic scale if you need to.

- **Gridlines: There should be no gridlines on the figure**. Go to **Chart Tools | Layout tab | Axis | Gridlines** and select **none** from each of the drop-down menus (Figure A2.15).

- **Legend: No legend (key) is required when there is only one line on the graph.** Under **Chart Tools | Layout | Labels | Legend** select **none**. You should not use a legend unless you have multiple lines of different color (or data point style) on the same graph. It is also suggested that you do not use lots of color unless you have good reason to. Pull the legend into the plot area to maximize the space that the chart takes up.

- **Data labels:** Data labels will clutter the plot area of your figure. In general, we do not use them for introductory biology.

- **Location**: By convention, figures are placed as close as possible to the location in the scientific paper where they are first

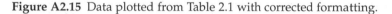

Figure A2.15 Data plotted from Table 2.1 with corrected formatting.

described. **Make all modifications and corrections to the graph in Excel before you copy it and paste it into Word**. Once it is imported into the Word document, it is no longer possible to make any changes (except to the size of the graph).

4.4 Manipulating Data within Chart Tools

If you want to change the range of the cells used to plot the graph, you can do so in **Chart Tools**. Select **Data** under the **Design tab** (Figure A2.16). This might be appropriate if you added or deleted data values in the spreadsheet. To add data to an existing figure, first enter the new data in cells on the spreadsheet. Select the chart. The currently included data will be highlighted. Extend the highlights to include the new data.

Add trendline. A trendline is a line that describes the general tendency of the data points. In Excel you can add any of six trendlines or regression lines (best-fit lines) to a data set. Excel automatically calculates the R-squared value and the equation of the line. The equation allows you to predict one variable when the other is known. The R-squared value gives you an indication of how well the line fits the data points (the closer to 1, the better the fit). See the section on "Trendlines" for situations when trendlines may be added to a data set. To add a trendline go to **Chart Tools tab | Layout | Analysis | Trendline** and select the appropriate trendline.

Figure A2.16 Data dialog box for formatting different parts of the graph.

4.5 Format Data Series

The symbols that science editors use are based on ease of recognition and good contrast in black and white journal publications. The criteria used by Excel to determine symbol hierarchy are not always clear to the user, especially since light-colored symbols are very hard to see on a white background.

To change the symbol style and/or color in Excel, select the symbols on the chart and go to **Format | Shape Styles** (Figure A2.17). In this dialog box, you can then change the format of your lines and symbols (here called markers):

- Change the **Marker** (symbol) to a circle, triangle, or square by clicking the arrow in the Shape Styles box and **Marker Options| Types**. Select the desired symbol from the drop down, In **Marker Line Color** choose **Black**. In **Marker Fill** choose **No color** to make an open circle, triangle, or square; or **Black** to make a filled circle, triangle, or square.

Format axes. Use the criteria in Table A2.4 to check that the axes have been formatted correctly. If any changes need to be made, click any number on

Figure A2.17 Format Data Series Dialog box, which allows you to further edit the chart symbols.

either the *x*- or *y*-axis (depending on which axis needs to be changed). Then you can use any of the command functions in the Ribbon to edit the appearance of the axis.

Multiple lines on one set of axes. In some experiments it is desirable to compare the results from a number of different treatments. Plotting the data on one set of axes is often the most efficient way to convey this information. How many lines should you put on one set of axes? The CSE Manual recommends no more than 8, but use common sense. You should be able to follow each line individually, and the graph should not look cluttered.

Because there will be a multitude of lines on the figure, it is critical to identify the individual sets of data by means of labels or a legend. Excel will generate a legend for each graph, provided you enter the appropriate titles in the spreadsheet. This can be accomplished by entering a short title in the first row of each of the data columns. These titles will be used by Excel to generate the legend.

Let's say you monitored the production of an enzyme called beta-galactosidase by *E. coli* grown under different conditions. Every 10 min for 1 hr, you measured the absorbance (which represents the concentration of beta-galactosidase) in each culture condition. Time is the independent variable that will be plotted on the *x*-axis. According to Excel convention, therefore,

TABLE A2.4 Checklist for axis label format

CORRECT FORMAT	HOW TO ADJUST
Dependent variable on *y*-axis	See "Entering Data in Spreadsheet"
Independent variable on *x*-axis	See "Entering Data in Spreadsheet"
Range of values on axes is slightly larger than range of data values being plotted	Right-click on the axis that you want to change. Select Format Axis from the pop-up menu. If negative values are not appropriate for the quantity plotted, Min = 0.
Tick marks are left of the *y*-axis and below the *x*-axis	Right-click on the axis that you want to change. Select Format Axis from the pop-up menu.
Numbers should be the same size and should read horizontally	Right-click on the axis that you want to change. Select Format Axis from the pop-up menu.
Vertical axis labels read parallel to the *y*-axis (they should never read vertically downward)	Alignment tab	Text alignment Vertical: Center Orientation: 0 degrees
No borders or background	Right-click on the the plot area, then select Format Chart from the pop-up menu.

time should be entered in Column A. The next five columns will contain the absorbance data at each time for the five different conditions (Table A2.5).

- Enter the data in the spreadsheet. Select all of the entries (column headings as well as numbers) and go to **Insert tab | Charts**.

- Select the **Scatter | Scatter with Straight Lines and Markers.**

- Make sure the data series is in **Columns**.

- Follow the Lab Report Guidelines mentioned earlier in the chapter to make the graph simple and clear. Your graph should look something like Figure A2.18.

Multiple trendlines on one set of axes This is similar to the previous example, except that the lines are trendlines, instead of smoothed or straight lines connecting the data points. Table A2.6 shows sample data for an experiment in which enzyme (catalase) activity was measured for different combinations of inhibitor (hydroxylamine) and substrate (hydrogen peroxide) concentrations. Column A gives the values for the x-axis (1/[H2O2] (M)),

TABLE A2.5 Sample data for beta-galactosidase production in *E. coli* grown under five different conditions

	A	B	C	D	E	F
1	Time (min)	Mutant, Gly	WT, Gly	WT, Gly IPTG	WT, Glu	WT, Glu IPTG
2	0	2	0.205	0.1	0.04	0.044
3	10	2	0.265	0.88	0.095	0.174
4	20	2	0.406	1.4	0.2	0.214
5	30	2	0.351	2	0.23	0.3
6	40	2	0.386	2	0.33	0.442
7	50	2	0.56	2	0.35	0.468
8	60	2	0.67	2	0.42	0.91

while Columns B–E give the data points for the y-axis (1/units of product formed • sec–1). Each column (line on the graph) represents one inhibitor concentration, which you enter in Row 1 for Columns B–E. These short titles are used by Excel to generate the legend.

Figure A2.18 Beta-galactosidase production in *E. coli* grown under five different conditions. The mutant strain, which produces a non-functional repressor protein, was grown in glycerol. The wild-type strain was grown in glycerol or glucose, with or without the addition of IPTG (a lactose analog) at $t = 0$ min.

1. Enter the data in the spreadsheet. *Note:* The column titles must begin with a non-numerical character such as I =; otherwise Excel confuses the number and percent symbol for a formula. Select all of the entries (column headings as well as numbers) and select **Insert tab | Charts** and select **Scatter with only Markers**.

2. Make sure the data series is in **Columns**.

3. Make modifications to the following Lab Report Guidelines (Section 4.3 of this Appendix).

4. Now we want to have Excel draw a linear trendline for each of the data sets to create a chart that looks like Figure A2.19. Select one of the symbols from each data set and go to **Chart Tools | Layout tab| Analysis | Trendline | Linear Trendline**.

5. Click **More Trendline Options**. Click the box next to **Display equation on chart**. The equations allow you to determine whether all the lines have a common y-intercept, a common x-intercept, or neither. This information is used to determine whether hydroxylamine is a competitive or noncompetitive inhibitor in this reaction.

6. Select **OK**. The resulting figure will look something like Figure A2.19.

7. Since the "Linear" entries in the legend are meaningless, click the entire legend and then **single-click each of these text boxes** (to activate the frame), and then press the **Delete** key. Drag the legend inside the axes. Drag the legend inside the axes, and remove the I =.

The resulting final graph will then look like Figure A2.20.

TABLE A2.6 Effect of hydroxylamine concentration on catalase activity for different concentrations of hydrogen peroxide

	A	B	C	D	E
1	1/[H2O2] (M)	I = 0%	I = 0.0025%	I = 0.025%	I = 0.25%
2	7.14	66.3	60.74	93.34	130.17
3	3.45	39.66	31.3	72.45	114.77
4	0.74	33.77	32.97	48.36	98.76
5	0.34	13.63	14.99	16.81	31.02

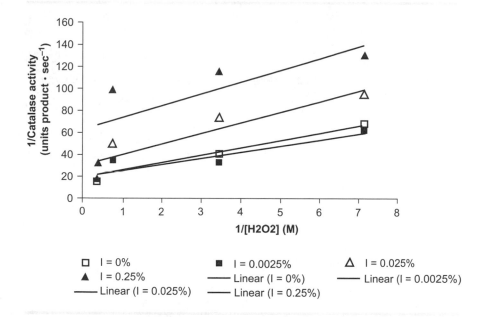

Figure A2.19 Effect of hydroxylamine concentration on catalase activity at different substrate concentrations. See Figure A2.20 for final form (note the location of the legend in both figures).

Figure A2.20 Effect of hydroxylamine concentration on catalase activity at different substrate concentrations.

PREPARING ORAL PRESENTATIONS WITH MICROSOFT POWERPOINT

Microsoft PowerPoint allows you to create a slide show containing text, graphics, and even animations. PowerPoint also allows you to make poster presentations. This can be done by making one large slide or several small slides arranged in a particular manner. The menus in PowerPoint parallel those in Microsoft Word, so if you are already familiar with Word, learning PowerPoint should not be difficult.

The screen drops in this appendix are for PowerPoint 2007. Path notation for reaching a particular command or option is shown relative to a command on the menu bar, toolbar, or task bar. For example, **View | Toolbars | Drawing** means "Click the View button (on the menu bar), then select Toolbars, and then click Drawing."

1. Starting PowerPoint

To start PowerPoint, click the **PowerPoint** button on the taskbar at the bottom of your screen. Alternatively, click **Start | All Programs | Microsoft Office | Microsoft PowerPoint**. When you start up PowerPoint 2007, a new presentation will be opened for you. If you are making a presentation in PowerPoint for the first time, click **Create a New Presentation Using Blank Presentation**. If you've already made a presentation and want to revise it, click the office button in the upper left corner of the screen. You will see a list of recent documents. If your file is not listed, select **Open** to browse your computer for the appropriate file. If you are working on a file and would like to open a new presentation click the office button and select **New**.

PowerPoint 2007 has a new style and organization of commands from previous versions of PowerPoint. Instead of menus, most of the commands are housed in a set of tabs that make up the Ribbon. The Ribbon is the panel on the top of the screen that contains the command buttons and icons (Fig-

(A)

(B)

Figure A3.1 A. The Ribbon containing command icons and buttons. B. Office Button and Quick Access Toolbar.

ure A3.1A). In the upper left corner, the File menu is replaced by the Office button. Next to the Office button is the Quick access toolbar which contains commonly used commands such as save, undo, and redo.

2. Slide Format

The normal view in PowerPoint 2007 shows a screen split into three panes (Figure A3.2):

- Outline of your presentation on the left
- Current slide on the right
- Speaker notes below the current slide

Under the Home tab there is a Slides box that will allow you to add new slides and choose layouts. Selecting Layout will open a selection of layouts for your current slide. The layouts range from text only to combinations of text and visual aid (table, graph, or image) to visual aid only. Selecting the New Slide icon will continue to open slides in the layout that you have chosen. Selecting the "new slide" button will allow you to quickly choose a layout and open a slide in the layout you prefer.

Type the text into the placeholders in the current slide (Figure A3.3). The same text will appear in the outline to the left so that later you can rearrange the text or the slides if desired (see the section on "Revising and Polishing Presentations").

2.1 Sample Presentation

The sample PowerPoint presentation we are using here is about a laboratory exercise in which a novel recombinant DNA, made of a plasmid

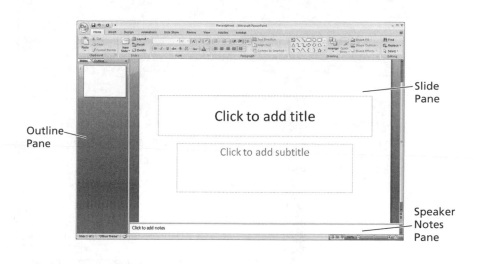

Figure A3.2 A new slide in PowerPoint 2007 in Normal view.

(pGEM) and a fragment of a virus that infects monkeys (SV40), was analyzed by agarose gel electrophoresis. Six different recombinant DNAs are possible, each one with the same plasmid (pGEM), but with a different SV40 insert. Since the SV40 inserts are all different sizes, and since agarose gel electrophoresis separates DNA fragments based on size, the goal of the exercise was to determine which of the six possible SV40 inserts was contained in the unknown recombinant DNA.

pGEM and SV40 were joined using a restriction enzyme called *Hin*dIII. In the lab exercise, the recombinant DNA was digested (cut apart) with *Hin*dIII, separating the DNA into its two components. The sample was then run on a gel, with the SV40 fragment migrating farther than the pGEM fragment because of its smaller size. By comparing the distance migrated by the SV40 fragment with a standard marker DNA, the identity of the SV40 fragment (based on its size) can be determined.

2.2 Creating a Title

To insert a title slide, click the **Title Slide Layout** under the **Home** tab. If this presentation were a lab report, a possible title might be "Analysis of

Figure A3.3 Text typed in the placeholders of the slide also appears in the outline to the left.

recombinant DNA consisting of pGEM and SV40 using agarose gel electrophoresis." For an oral presentation to students who have all done the lab exercise, however, this long, descriptive title is not likely to generate excitement. **Know your audience and capture their interest immediately with a short, catchy title** such as the one in Figure A3.3.

2.3 Adding New Slides

Presentations in biology usually follow the Introduction-Body-Closing format. In the **Introduction**, the speaker guides the audience from information that is generally familiar to them to new information, which is the focus (**Body**) of the talk. The take-home message for the audience is given in the **Closing**.

To make the next slide, click the **New Slide** button under the **Home** tab. Clicking the words underneath will allow you to quickly choose the slide layout. Selecting the layout button will allow you to change the layout of the current slide. A bulleted list works well if you want to give an overview of your talk first (Figure A3.4A). Each bulleted item should be a short phrase with keywords or key points, not full sentences. The phrases themselves should be informative but interesting for your audience. A good rule of thumb is to use no more than six words per bullet and no more than six bulleted items on one slide.

To delete a slide, display the slide you want to delete, and click **Delete** in the slides box under the Home tab.

2.4 Formatting Text

Just as in Microsoft Word, you can apply formatting such as font, font size, bold, italics, underline, color, and alignment **to selected words or lines in a single slide** by using the buttons on the Font box under the Home tab. Select the text to be formatted by holding down the left mouse button and dragging across the text block from the first character to the last. Release the mouse button and click the desired formatting button on the toolbar.

Clicking on the bottom right of the Font box will open the font dialog box. To **subscript or superscript text**, select the character(s) to be formatted, click the appropriate box under **Effects** in the Font dialog box. This dialog box also allows you to change **text color**.

A good rule of thumb is to use **no more than two fonts or colors**, and to use them only for emphasis. For example, boldfaced, italicized, larger sized, and colored text stands out against the default text.

To **insert symbols** (Greek letters, mathematical symbols, Wingdings, etc.), click the **Insert** tab and find the Symbol button in the Text box. Look for the desired symbol. For a uniform look, select the same font in the Symbol dialog window as the text font you are using in your PowerPoint presentation. It is not possible to make shortcut keys for symbols in PowerPoint, but if the symbols occur frequently in your presentation, you can copy and paste them to save yourself some keystrokes.

The **AutoCorrect** feature in Microsoft Word is also available in Power-Point. Click the **Office Button | Powerpoint Options | Proofing**. Not only is it useful for correcting spelling mistakes, it can be used to replace long chemical names with a simple keystroke combination and to italicize scientific names of organisms automatically. See Appendix 1, Section 4.6 for instructions on using the AutoCorrect feature.

If you want to make changes that **affect the text in every slide in the presentation**, see the section on "Slide Master and Title Master." The default

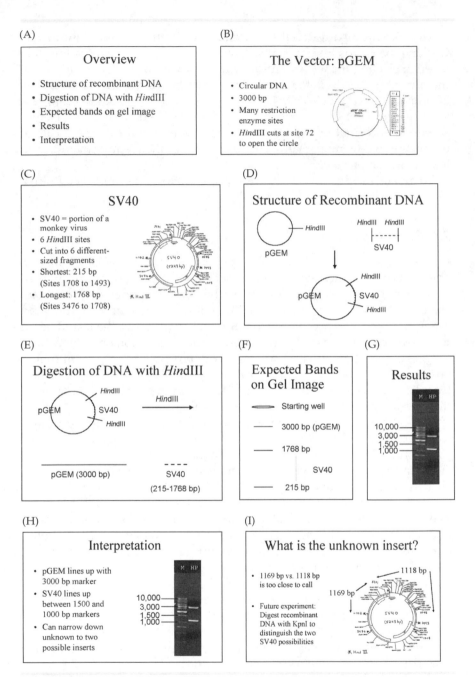

Figure A3.4 Slides with different combinations of text and visuals in a presentation about recombinant DNA analysis using agarose gel electrophoresis.

font size (44 pt for titles and 32 pt for text) is designed to be large enough to be read even in the back of an average-sized classroom, so don't reduce font size to get more information on the slide. Instead, keep the wording concise.

3. Adding Images

A presentation with only text slides rarely gets your message across as effectively as one that combines text and visual aids. Visual aids take time to make or find, but they are worth the effort to capture and maintain audience interest.

The basic slide layout options are:

- Text only
- Text and a visual
- Visual only

While PowerPoint offers you many more than three slide layouts to choose from, you will find that most of the layouts are redundant. You can actually insert a visual into any placeholder in any of the slide layouts, but you can only type text in layouts that have text boxes. **To delete the existing placeholder box**, simply *right click* the placeholder and select **Cut**. Figures A3.4B, C, H, and I are slides from the sample presentation, which have **both text and a visual**. Figures A3.4D, E, F, and G are slides with **just a visual**, and Figure A3.3 (the title slide) and Figure A3.4A are **text-only** slides.

Follow the instructions in the text placeholders to add a title or text. To insert a visual, you have several options.

3.1 Copy and Paste

Click the image from a Word, Excel, or other file and then **Home** and **Copy** (🖳) from the clipboard box. (You can also use the keyboard shortcut Ctrl+C, or right mouse button menu to copy). Click the desired location in the PowerPoint slide and click **Home | Paste** (🖳), keyboard shortcut Ctrl+V, or right mouse button to paste. Make sure the text (if any) in the visual is large and legible (in Figure A3.4B and C, the text on the actual slide meets these criteria). To resize the image:

- Click the image to display the selection handles around the frame
- Position the mouse pointer over a handle (small circle or square at the perimeter of the image) in one of the corners to display a two-headed arrow
- Hold down the left mouse button and drag the frame to the desired size, and then release the mouse button

To reposition the image, position the cursor over the image to display crossed arrows, hold down the left mouse button, drag the image to the desired location, and release the mouse button.

3.2 Insert | Picture

The illustration box under the Insert tab has different options for picture sources (Clip Art, Picture From File, etc.). PowerPoint readily accepts .jpg, .gif, .bmp and other standard image file formats. The gel image in Figure A3.4G and H was added to the slide using the Picture command from the Insert tab. **Resize and reposition if necessary** (see the section on "Copy and Paste"). To crop the picture, select it, and then click the **Crop** button in the Size box under the format tab. **Format | Picture** from the menu bar. You can crop the picture precisely by entering numbers for height and width in the Size box.

3.3 Drawing Toolbar

To add simple graphics to your slide, go to the Drawing box in the Home tab (Figure A3.5). **To add a line,** for example, click the line within the Drawing box toolbar to display crosshairs. Position the mouse pointer on the slide where you want the line to start, hold down the left mouse button, drag to where you want the line to end, and release the mouse button.

   To change the angle or length of the line, click the line and then position the mouse pointer over one of the end points of the line to display a two-headed arrow. Hold down the left mouse button, drag to where you want the line to end, and release the mouse button.

   To change the location of the line, click the line and then position the mouse pointer over the line to display crossed arrows. Hold down the left mouse button, drag the line to the desired location, and release the mouse button. For more precise positioning, click the line to display the selection

Figure A3.5 Drawing toolbox for making simple graphics.

handles. From the menu bar, select **Format | AutoShape |Layout** and click the **Advanced** button. Change the numbers to place the line exactly where you want it.

   To format the line, click the line to display the selection handles. From the Ribbon, select the **Format** tab to change the appearance of the line. The Sizing box will allow you to size it precisely.

   To add text to your drawing, click the **Text Box** button in the Text box under the Insert tab. Position the mouse pointer where you want the text box to appear, hold down the left mouse button, drag to enlarge the text box to the size you think you'll need (you can resize it later), and release the mouse button. Now you can type the text inside the box. Font type and font size can be changed by selecting the text and by using the commands on Font box under the Home tab. To format the text box itself, click the text box to display the selection handles on the frame. Click **Paragraph | Text Direction | More options** under the Home tab. This opens a dialog box that allows you to change the appearance, size, position, and word wrapping of the text box.

   If individual objects make up a graphic, then it may make sense to group them as a unit. Grouping allows you to copy, move, or format all of the objects in the graphic at one time. **To group individual objects into one unit,** click each object while holding down the **Shift** key. Release the **Shift** key, click the Format tab and then **Group** in the **Arrange** box. You can also right click the objects and select the **group** option. One set of selection handles surrounds the entire unit when the individual objects are grouped. To ungroup, simply select the group, click the **Format** tab and click **Ungroup** from the group drop-down menu (Figure A3.6). For an example of line drawings that were created using the Drawing toolbar, see Figures A3.4D–F.

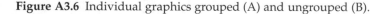

Figure A3.6 Individual graphics grouped (A) and ungrouped (B).

4. Adding a Table

To make a table that spans the entire slide, click **Insert | Table** or click **Home | Layout** and choose an Office theme with content. Then when you click the placeholder, a dialog box asks you to choose the number of columns and rows for the table. To insert a table into a one-column slide, click **Insert | Table** and enter the desired number of columns and rows. A table then appears in the slide, and all of the cells are the same size. After typing text in any of the cells, you can change the size of the cells manually. To do this, position the mouse pointer on one of the horizontal (⟊) or vertical lines (⟊). Hold down the left mouse button, move the pointer to adjust the row or column size, and then release the mouse button. There are other formatting options located on the Tables and Borders floating toolbar, such as splitting and merging cells and inserting or deleting columns or rows.

Small tables can also be added to slides with two-column format. Click one of the placeholders and select **Insert | Table** from the menu bar. Enter the number of columns and rows, and click **OK**.

5. Adding a Graph

If you are already familiar with making graphs in Microsoft Excel, then the easiest way to add graphs to a PowerPoint presentation is to copy and paste as follows:

- Make a graph in Excel (see Appendix 2).
- Single-click the **Chart Area** to activate the graph. Click **Copy**.
- In PowerPoint, click **Home | New Slide** and choose a layout suitable for the graph.
- Click **Paste**. Resize and reposition the graph as needed (see the section on "Copy and Paste").

6. Navigating among Slides

There are several ways to move from one slide to another when preparing a presentation (Figure A3.7): If **Normal view** is selected (click **View** tab and click **Normal** in the **Presentation Views window**):

- Click the **Page Up** or **Page Down** key on the keyboard.
- Use the vertical scroll bar on the right-hand side of the Slide pane.
- Inside the scroll bar, drag the scroll box up or down to move backwards or forwards through the presentation.

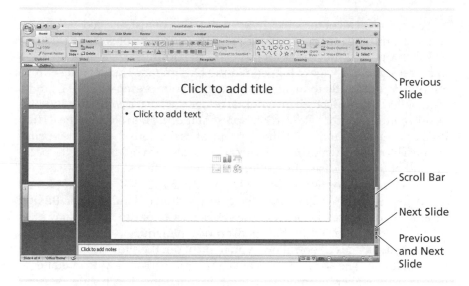

Figure A3.7 Ways to navigate among slides in Normal view.

- Click the **Preuious Slide** or **Next Slide** arrow buttons to move from slide to slide.
- On the left-hand side of the screen is the Outline pane. Click the text on the slide you want to display. There are two tabs on the Outline pane: **Outline** (text) and **Slides** (thumbnails). Choose the view you prefer.

In **Slide Sorter view** in the **Presentation views** window, single-click the desired slide to select it. Double-click it to edit the contents in Normal view.

7. Saving and Printing Presentations

To save a presentation for the first time, click the Office button and save in the drop-down menu. You can also select the **Saue** icon from the Quick access toolbar located next to the Office button. Do not wait until you are finished making the entire presentation to save the file. Save it after you have made the first slide. Choose a meaningful name for the file; Power-Point automatically saves the file as a "Presentation," with the .ppt extension. At the top of the dialog box, click the down arrow next to the **Saue in** text box to select the location (drive, folder, sub-folder) where you want to save the file.

You can print all of the slides in a presentation or just selected slides. You can also print the outline, handouts, and the speaker notes.

When printing the **Slides**, first specify the desired size and orientation in by selecting the Page setup icon in the Design tab. The default settings are fine if you decide to make overheads for your presentation (e.g., if the room where you will be giving your talk does not have a computer and projection equipment for a PowerPoint presentation). Then click on the **Office Button** and **Print** and make the appropriate selections there. When printing on a black-and-white printer, select Grayscale to avoid printing the background of the slides (see the section on "Special Effects").

The **Handouts** option is useful for printing 1, 2, 3, 4, 6, or 9 slides on one page. Select the orientation of the page (portrait or landscape) in **Design | Page Setup**. Select the order of the slides (across or down the page) after selecting Print in the Office button drop-down menu.

The **Notes Pages** option allows you to print out the slide and the speaker notes below it. The speaker notes are comparable to notecards in that they help you remember the important points to make about each slide. By sticking to the script, you are likely to stay within your time limit and avoid getting sidetracked. As with Handouts, the orientation of the Notes pages is selected in **Design | Page Setup**. To print out two or more Notes pages on one sheet of paper, click **Office Button | Print | Properties** and choose the desired number of **Pages per Sheet**.

8. Revising and Polishing Presentations

PowerPoint provides **multiple views** for displaying a presentation: Normal, Slide Sorter, Notes Page, and Slide Show. You can switch views two ways:

- Click the **View** tab and select a different view from the Presentation Views window.
- Click one of the buttons in the lower left corner of the screen

Slide Sorter view is useful for evaluating the overall appearance of a presentation, because it displays all of the slides in a presentation in miniature, complete with formatting (see the section on "Special Effects"). You cannot edit the contents of an individual slide in Slide Sorter view, but you can rearrange the slides.

Click **View | Slide Sorter** to change to Slide Sorter view. To select a slide to move, copy, add, or delete, single-click it with the right mouse button. To edit the contents of the slide in Normal view, double-click it.

8.1 Moving Slides

To move a slide, position the mouse pointer on the slide you want to move, hold down the left mouse button and drag the vertical line to a new location between slides, and release the mouse button. The slide now appears at its new position. You can also move a slide using the **Cut** function in the Clipboard box under the Home tab, clicking at the new insertion point, and clicking the **Paste** button in the Clipboard box.

To move a group of adjacent slides, click the first slide in the group, hold down **Shift** on the keyboard, and click the last slide in the group. All slides will be marked with a highlighted border. Hold down the left mouse button, drag the vertical line to a new insertion point between slides, and release the mouse button. The group of slides appears at its new position. As with a single slide, you can also use the **Cut** and **Paste** commands on the Clipboard box under the Home tab.

To move a group of nonadjacent slides, follow the procedure for adjacent slides, but hold down **Ctrl** instead of **Shift** on the keyboard. The slides appear in the same consecutive order at the new location.

8.2 Adding and Deleting Slides

To add a new slide, click the slide that you want the new slide to follow. Then click **New Slide** from the Home tab and choose a slide layout. Click **OK** and a new slide is inserted in the presentation. Click on the new slide to add content.

To delete an unwanted slide, single-click the slide and press **Delete** on the keyboard. To correct the deletion, click the **Undo** button from the Quick Access toolbar on the top of the screen.

8.3 Copying Slides

To copy a slide, click the slide you want to copy and then the Copy button from the Clipboard box under the Home tab. Click the insertion point between slides and then click **Paste** from the Clipboard box. You can also copy a slide from another presentation using this method. If you want the duplicate slide to immediately follow the original, click the slide to be copied and select **Duplicate** from the Paste drop-down menu in the Home tab. The duplicate will be inserted automatically after the original. To change the layout on the duplicate, simply single-click the duplicate slide, click **Layout** in the Slides box under the Home tab and select a new layout for the slide. This method was used to make Figure A3.4H from Figure A3.4G.

Slides can also be rearranged in the Outline pane in Normal view using the same procedures just described.

8.4 Spell Check

Don't let an otherwise interesting and well-organized presentation be ruined by typos on the slides. As with Microsoft Word, PowerPoint offers three ways to correct spelling and grammar:

- AutoCorrect
- Automatic spelling and grammar checker
- Manual, systematic spelling and grammar check See Appendix 1, Section 3.4 for instructions on using these spell checkers.

8.5 Special Effects

While your presentation will be evaluated primarily on content and organization, appearance definitely affects your instructor's state of mind. Table A3.1 gives some recommendations for the appearance of your slide show.

There is nothing wrong with a well-rehearsed black-and-white slide show. On the other hand, we are so accustomed to colorful animations and interactive computer programs that we have come to expect this level of entertainment in all aspects of our daily lives. While scientists view themselves primarily as conveyors of information rather than entertainers, adding some well-chosen special effects to our presentations may help get the message across more effectively.

TABLE A3.1 Presentation tips

DO	DON'T
Keep the wording simple	Write every word you're going to say on the slide
Make the text large and legible	Vary the background or use distracting slide transitions and sound effects
Strive for a consistent look (use the same font and format for each slide)	Include tables when you can show the trend better with a graph
Include visual aids to provide both visual and auditory information	Talk endlessly without referring to a visual
Allow enough time for each slide	Rush through the slides without mentioning the take-home message about each one

Background. An easy way to change the background of your slides is to add color or apply a design template to an existing presentation. Open your presentation (see the section on "Starting PowerPoint") and click **View | Slide Sorter**. This view allows you to see how changes affect the entire slide show.

PowerPoint offers a wide variety of design templates that give your slides a uniform and professional look. The Design tab allows you to change the appearance of your slides. Under the Design tab there are a number of templates to choose from. Templates with a light background make the room much brighter during the actual presentation, which has the dual advantage of keeping the audience awake and allowing you to see your listeners' faces. Many professional speakers, however, prefer white text on a dark background because the text appears larger. Whatever your preference, choose a template that reflects your style, is appropriate for the topic, and complements the content of the individual slides. Avoid using light text on light backgrounds and dark text on dark backgrounds.

Slide Master and Title Master. The Slide Master controls the **appearance of the text and objects** in every slide except the title slide. The Title Master allows you to apply a format to the title slide, which is different from that in the rest of the slides.

Note: If you have not applied a design template to your presentation, the Title Master command is unavailable and changes made in the Slide Master also affect the title slide.

You can modify the Slide Master and Title Master at any time—before, during, or after making the first draft of your presentation. Under the View tab select the Slide Master button from the Presentation Views box. You will see the default design (Figure A3.8) or the currently applied design template. There you can also edit the title master.

The Font box under the Home tab will allow you to change the font, font style, font size, or font color. The paragraph box contains a Bullet icon that will allow you to change the bullet. Click anywhere on the bulleted line and select the arrow button next to the icon. You can also insert objects such as clip art or images into the Title Area or Object Area. Click the **Insert** tab and then make the appropriate selection from the Illustration box. **The changes affect every slide in the presentation, except the title slide**.

The color scheme of the Slide Master is determined by the selected design template to ensure that the text color harmonizes with, and is legible against, the background color. **When you change the Slide Master, however, you override the default color scheme**. In other words, the text colors you specify in the Slide Master are applied instead of the color scheme's text col-

Figure A3.8 Default Slide Master (no design template is applied).

ors. Strive to maintain good contrast whenever you modify the text and background colors.

Adding Headers and Footers. The three boxes at the bottom of the Slide Master allow you to enter the date and time, a custom footer, and the page number. While it is not customary to display this information during a slide show, it may be handy to have it on the printed slides if they are used as handouts.

To turn off footer options for a slide show (Figure A3.9A):

- Click the **Header and Footer** button from the Insert tab to display the **Header and Footer** dialog box.
- On the **Slide** tab, clear the Date and Time, Slide Number, and Footer check boxes.

Even if you've added a date, custom footer, or page number to the slide master or title master, these will not be displayed on the slide. To display

Figure A3.9 Footers defined in the slide master or title master can be turned off (A) or on (B) on the Slide tab in the Header and Footer dialog box.

footers defined in the slide master or title master on the printed slide itself (Figure A3.9B):

- Click **Insert | Header and Footer** on the menu bar to display the Header and Footer dialog box.

- On the **Slide** tab, select the Date and Time, Slide Number, and Footer check boxes.

- Click **Apply to All** to print this information on every slide.

- Click **Office Button | Print** and select **Slides** from the **Print What** drop-down list.

- Make any other selections in the **Print** dialog box and then click **OK**.

Footers defined in the slide master or title master only appear on the slide (if you have made the appropriate selections), not in the footer of a Handouts or Notes page (to print out Handouts or Notes pages, click **Office Button | Print | Print What**). You may want to define a header and footer on these printed materials, which is different from the footer you have on the slides themselves.

To define a different header and footer, follow these steps:

- Click **Insert | Header and Footer** from the menu bar to display the **Header and Footer** dialog box.

- On the **Slide** tab, clear the Date and Time, Slide Number, and Footer check boxes.

- On the **Notes and Handouts** tab, select the relevant check boxes (Figure A3.10). The default settings are date and time displayed in the upper right corner and the page number in the lower right corner. A custom header and footer can be entered in the respective boxes if desired.

- Click **Apply to All** to print the selected information on every page.

- Click **Office Button | Print** and select **Handouts** or **Notes Pages** from the **Print What** drop-down list.

- Make any other selections in the **Print** dialog box and then click **OK**.

Slide Transitions. **Transitions** affect the way slides appear in a slide show. To see how your presentation looks without slide transitions, click the first slide in **Slide Sorter view** or display the first slide in Normal view and then change the view to Slide Show (using **View |Slide Show** or the corresponding button in the lower left corner of the screen). The first slide will stay on the screen until you click the left mouse button, press **Enter**, or press

Figure A3.10 Header and Footer dialog box allows you to print date and time, page number, and a custom header and footer on Handouts and Notes pages.

the space bar on the keyboard to advance to the next slide. The slides in the presentation are displayed sequentially unless you press the **Esc** key to end the show, click a button on the Slide Show toolbar in the lower left corner of the screen, or right click and choose an option from the menu.

To explore different transitions click on the Animation tab. There you will see a set of icons representing a number of animations you can use for your presentation. Placing your mouse over an icon will allow you to preview the animation (Figure A3.11). **If you choose to add Slide Transition Effects to your presentation, make sure they do not detract from the content!**

To apply a basic transition effect to a slide, click the slide, and then select an effect by clicking one of the icons in the Transition to this Slide box. Clicking the arrows next to the icons will open a drop-down menu containing more possible transitions to choose from. You will see an instant preview of the effect. You can click the preview button in the Ribbon to replay the effect (Figure A3.12).

To apply a single effect to all the slides, in the Editing box under the Home tab click **Select | Select All** and then choose an effect from the **Transition to this Slide** drop-down menu. To clear the Select All option, click between any two slides or after the last slide. **To apply a single effect only to selected slides,** hold down **Shift** or **Ctrl** on the keyboard (see the section on "Moving Slides") and select the slides.

To modify the Slide Transition Effect selected for a slide, refer to the right-hand side of the Transition to this Slide box. There you can change the effect, the speed for the effect, and how long the slide is displayed on the screen. You can even add sound to the slide. After you have selected the desired options, they will be applied to the current slide. Click **Apply to All** to apply them to all the slides in the presentation.

Multimedia Files. Movie and video clips, music, and sounds may enhance your presentation. To insert multimedia files, first make sure you are not in Slide Sorter view. Then select **Movie** or **Sound** from the Media Clips box under the Insert tab. A dialog box asks if you want the clip to play auto-

Figure A3.11 In PowerPoint 2000, the Slide Sorter toolbar allows you to select effects for slide transitions.

Figure A3.12 Transition effect selected for Slide 1 is "Blinds Horizontal." To view the effect, click the Transition effect icon or the Animation Preview button.

matically when you reach that slide in the slide show or only when you click it. After selecting **Yes** or **No**, a screen shot of your video will appear.

Not all movie and video clips can be imported into PowerPoint. Some require the installation of additional software such as QuickTime for the clip to work. If you are having problems playing movie or sound clips in PowerPoint, ask someone in computer services for help.

9. Delivering Your Presentation

A PowerPoint presentation can be "delivered" electronically by attaching it to an e-mail, but most presentations are delivered in person. Do your homework and find out what audio-visual equipment is available in the room where you will give your talk. If you only have a chalkboard, just print out the speaker notes. If you'll have access to an overhead projector and screen, print out the slides and make transparencies. These printing options are explained in the section on "Saving and Printing Presentations."

Practice a few slides well in advance so that if a problem arises, you will have time to get help from the system administrator.

9.1 Running the Show

To deliver a PowerPoint slide show, you'll need a computer and projection equipment as well as a screen on which to display the slides. If the presentation room does not have this equipment, ask your host if he/she can provide it or, if you are affiliated with a college or university, you may be able to borrow a laptop computer and projector for your presentation.

There are several ways to run a PowerPoint presentation:

- From a Web server
- From a disk or CD on a computer at the presentation site
- From your laptop computer

To run a presentation from a Web server, first find out if you have access to the Internet at the presentation site. If so, save your file as a Web page and write down the address of the Web folder. Similarly, if your college or university has networked computers, you can prepare your presentation on a networked computer in your room, for example, save the file in your Private Space, and then access the file from another networked computer in the room where you will hold your talk.

If the presentation site has a computer, but it is not hooked up to the Internet, save your .ppt file on a removable disk and carry it with you. Ask your host if PowerPoint is installed on the presentation room's computer. If so, just insert the disk or CD, start PowerPoint, open your .ppt file, and click the **Slide Show** button in the lower left corner of the screen.

If the presentation site's computer does not have PowerPoint installed on it, you may be able to install PowerPoint from a set of disks you bring with you. To learn more about this option, ask your system administrator.

If you have a laptop computer, make sure PowerPoint is installed on it, and then save your .ppt file on the hard drive. At the presentation site, start PowerPoint, open the .ppt file, and click the **Slide Show** button in the lower left corner of the screen to begin your presentation.

9.2 Navigating among Slides during a Slide Show

Click the **Slide Show** button in the lower left corner of the screen to begin your presentation. If you have not specified a time for the slides to advance automatically (see the section on "Slide Transitions"), the first slide stays on the screen until you click the left mouse button, or press **Enter** or the

Figure A3.13 Options for navigating among slides during a slide show. Clicking the Go to Slide command on the Slide Show toolbar opens further menus that allow you to select and display a specific slide. The toolbar also has arrows to go forward and backward, a pointer button, and a slide button for navigation options.

space bar on the keyboard. A cordless mouse allows you to change slides from anywhere in the room.

There are two ways to change slides with the mouse:

- Click a button on the Slide Show toolbar in the lower left corner of the screen (Figure A3.13).

- Click the right mouse button to display the main menu of navigation options.

To end a slide show, press the **Esc** key on the keyboard or select **End Show** from the pop-up menu.

BIBLIOGRAPHY

Bregman A. 1996. Laboratory investigations in cell and molecular biology. Rev. 3rd ed. New York: John Wiley & Sons. 336 p.

Calabria J, Burke D. 1997. Microsoft Word 97 exam guide. Indianapolis: QUE Corp.

Corrections to Publications: Corrections to Scientific Style and Format (6th ed.) Updated June 2000 Available at <http://www. councilscienceeditors.org/ publications/ corrections6th.cfm> Accessed 2004 Oct 20.

D'Arcy J. 1998. Technically Speaking: A Guide for Communicating Complex Information. Columbus: Battelle Press. 270 p.

Fegert F, Hergenröder F, Mechelke G, Rosum K. 2002. Projektarbeit: Theorie und Praxis. Stuttgart: Landesinstitut für Erziehung und Unterricht Stuttgart. 226 p.

Glenn W. 2000. Word 2000 in a nutshell. Sebastopol, CA: O'Reilly & Associates, Inc. 491 p.

Hacker D. 1997. A pocket style manual. 2nd ed. Boston: Bedford Books. 185 p.

Hailman JP, Strier KB. 1997. Planning, proposing, and presenting science effectively. Cambridge: Cambridge University Press. 150 p.

Harnack A, Kleppinger E. 2001. Online! A reference guide to using internet sources. Boston: Bedford/St. Martins. 260 p.

Information Services and Resources, Bucknell University. 2004. Evaluating Websites as Sources. Available at <http://www.bucknell.edu/Library_computing/Doing_ Research/Start_Your_Research_Here/Evaluating_Sources/Website.html> Accessed 2006 May 1.

Jones A, Reed R, Weyers J. 1994. Practical skills in biology. London: Longman Scientific & Technical. 292 p.

Lannon JM. 2000. Technical Communication, 8th ed. New York: Addison Wesley Longman, Inc. 680 p.

Light RJ. 2001. Making the most of college: Students speak their minds. Cambridge, MA: Harvard University Press. 242 p.

Lunsford A. 2002. The everyday writer. 2nd ed. Boston: Bedford/St. Martin's. 534 p.

Lunsford A, Connors R. 1999. Easy writer: A pocket guide. Boston: Bedford/St. Martin's. 266 p.

Lunsford A, Connors R. 1995. The new St. Martin's handbook. 3rd ed. Boston: Bedford/St. Martin's. 797 p.

McMillan VE. 1997. Writing papers in the biological sciences. 2nd ed. Boston: Bedford Books. 197 p.

Moore DS. 2000. The basic practice of statistics. 2nd ed. New York: W. H. Freeman and Company. 619 p.

Palmer-Stone D. Last revised July 31, 2001. How to Read University Texts or Journal Articles. Counselling Services, University of Victoria, Victoria, BC, Canada. Available at <http://www.coun.uvic. ca/learn/program/hndouts/Readtxt.html> Accessed 2004 Oct 20.

Pechenik JA. 2004. A Short Guide to Writing About Biology, 5th ed. New York: Pearson/Longman. 302 p.

Peterson SM. 1999. Council of Biology Editors guidelines No. 2: Editing science graphs. Reston, VA: Council of Biology Editors. 34 p.

Peterson SM, Eastwood S. 1999. Council of Biology Editors guidelines No. 1: Posters and poster sessions. Reston, VA: Council of Biology Editors. 15 p.

Sagman SW. 1999. Running Microsoft PowerPoint 2000. Redmond, WA: Microsoft Press. 553 p.

Samuels ML, Witmer JA. 1999. Statistics for the life sciences. 2nd ed. Upper Saddle River, NJ: Prentice Hall. 683 p.

Style Manual Committee, Council of Science Editors. 2006. Scientific style and format: The CSE manual for authors, editors, and publishers. 7th ed. Reston, VA: Council of Science Editors in cooperation with the Rockefeller University Press. 680 p.

The University of Reading, IT Services. April 21, 2006. Equations and fields in Microsoft Word 2003 <http://www.rdg.ac.uk/ITS/info/training/notes/word/equations/> Accessed 2006 Aug 3.

Utts JM, Heckard RF. 2002. Mind on statistics. Pacific Grove, CA: Duxbury Press. 592 p.

VanAlstyne JS. 1986. Professional and technical writing strategies. Upper Saddle River, NJ: Prentice Hall, Inc. 433 p.

Vodopich D, Moore R. 1996. Biology laboratory manual to accompany biology. 4th ed. Boston: WCB/McGraw-Hill. 510 p.

Vogt C. 2004. Creating Equations with Microsoft Word. Information Systems & Technology, University of Waterloo, Waterloo, Ontario Canada. Available at <http://ist.uwaterloo.ca/ec/equations/equation.html> Accessed 2004 Aug 7.

Woolsey JD. 1989. Combating poster fatigue: How to use visual grammar and analysis to effect better visual communications. Trends in Neuroscience 12(9): 325–332.

INDEX

Pages with a * indicate a table or figure.